Croutons and Cheese!

Rod Fleming

Published in 2016 by PlashMill Press, Friockheim, Scotland.

Copyright© 2016 Rod Fleming

All rights reserved.

All names in this publication have been changed to protect the identities of the real people.

ISBN: 978-0-9572612-4-2

All photographs and artwork: Rod Fleming

To my children, and to my mother. I love all of you more than I have ever been able to say. Forgive me.

Contents

Preface	1
The Bells	3
Spring, Slugs and Spliffs	7
P'tit Moulin Chicken	16
Wine and Such	20
Eye Trouble	23
The Drains	32
The Stove Story	46
Black Economy	49
Animal Anecdotes	55
The Firemen and the Flying Cat	59
The Throat Holder-Upper	62
Sandy Takes Down the Pine Tree	65
Flaming Old Daimler	72
Dee and the Birthday Cake	77
Poor Sweepie	86
Les Quattors Juillets	90
The Woman Whose Car Would Not Start	98
Kiki *la Gare*	101
The British Airmen	106
Bûcheron Barbu	110
The Green Beans and the Giant Courgettes	118
A Tale of Two Cheeses	126
A Bull in the Back Passage	135
Man-Trap!	143
Cops in France	145
Antoine's Pyrotechnical Delight	151
Lézards and *Lézardes* (A Riddle)	158
Dinner Parties and Escaped Cows	162
Les Stephans	167
Wine, Bread and Camembert	174
A Little History	178
The Boys Next Door	187
African Market	191

Green Poo	194
Monsters in P'tit Moulin	199
The Tomettes	205
Le Bol de Mariage	209
Postscript.	215

Preface

In the early years of the last decade of the twentieth century, the little village of P'tit Moulin, high in the Arrière-côte, that wild limestone country full of escarpments and high moors that looms above the rich and fertile plain of Bresse, was a sleepy place. Very few of the inhabitants had any money. P'tit Moulin lies at four hundred metres of elevation. It's too high up for the most lucrative agriculture of this part of the world, the production of wine, on which the citizens of Beaune, down on the plain, have grown fat and rich. Up here in the rolling and wooded hills a man must work hard to make the land pay; not to mention his wife and sons and daughters. Here is the cattle king, and no more so than the mighty Charolais. Fine eating a P'tit Moulin beast makes too, let me assure you.

Where the *viticulteurs* of the Côte d'Or drive themselves around in late-model four-by-fours, the standard mode of transport, at the time of which I write, amongst the farmers of P'tit Moulin, was a venerable Renault 4. This usually had all but the driver's seat removed, because that way you can get more bales in.

Some of the wealthier farmers had recently bought little Renault vans, which was in part a reflection of the slowly growing affluence of this forgotten corner of Old France. But it helped that *l'Administration* had, in its wisdom, decided to give 20,000 francs to the owners of cars more than eight years old if they would only scrap them and buy a new vehicle. Well, in P'tit Moulin that much money – tax fee and even better, from the State – was a windfall, believe you me, and no canny Moulinard was going to pass that one up. So a fleet of little new cars and vans had begun to appear. These remained delightfully neat and pristine, despite the rigours of the agricultural life.

How so, you may ask? Well, the Moulinards are a clever bunch – Celts to a man of course, who have successfully persisted through the invasions of Romans and Franks, to say nothing of the Germans, *mon Dieu*, and survival like that brings canniness with it. So although it was necessary to get a receipt for the old car from the scrap-merchant, there was nothing that prevented them from buying the car back again the next day. In fact all that changed hands was five hundred francs as a little present; the actual scrap value of the vehicle. The scrappy had the necessary paperwork to say he had bought the car for scrap, and that he had disposed of it as such. Simple.

The banged-up Renault 4 – which naturally, could no longer be registered, but when did a minor inconvenience like that stop anyone – went right on serving the needs of the farmer, transporting feed, bales, and calves around the place, while the nice shiny new car was kept for ferrying Madame to the shops in Autun. Even *l'Administration* was happy, for once, since, as far as it was concerned, the old heap it had paid to take off the road was, indeed, off the road. It was a very French compromise, one which respected the need to finesse the system to make it work properly.

Digression is a part of life in France. Indeed many would say that digression *is* life in France, so I make no bones about it; we shall be digressing frequently. And now, once you have provided yourself with a nice glass of Burgundy (I do hope you don't drink that Ozzie roo-water,) let me introduce you to *French Onion Soup 2: Croutons and Cheese!* In which the intrepid Fleming family rise once again to the challenges of living in a half-millennium old pile well lost in *la France profonde*, and observations and amusements based thereon.

We hope you enjoy yourselves.

The Bells

Do you know about the bells? No? Oh well, time to find out, now. In France, clock bells ring the hour twice, once a minute before the hour and once on the hour. So if you miscounted the first time round, you have no excuse the second. Marvellously rational, the French are.

Anyway, a while ago, something strange began to happen. Sometimes the bells would ring, and sometimes they wouldn't. Sometimes they would ring once when they were meant to ring twice, leaving those of us who got lost the first time round high and dry. Slowly, this got worse and worse, till they made no sense at all.

At first I thought Quasi must have been hitting the sauce or had had a bust-up with Esmeralda again, but then I remembered, no, our bells are automatic…well, kinda. A straw poll of the neighbours showed that I was not the only one who had noticed, which I must say was a great relief. It did lessen the probability that there was nothing wrong with the bells, it was just me going mad. Although there was always that suspicion at the back of my mind that maybe my neighbours were just as mad as I…

Well, anyway, one day at around mid-morning they really did go ballistic. Or perhaps *bellistic*. I am not above punning, you know, so those of weak constitution ought perhaps to have a little drink handy. For medicinal purposes.

Anyway, on the occasion in hand, bells of all descriptions began ringing like Judgement Day had finally arrived; though why it was being announced in our sleepy neck of the woods was beyond me. I should have thought Kentucky more appropriate.

At first I thought someone had died, and then, no, it can't be that, must be a wedding…a birth? A Christening? Christmas? Hello, why did the clock bell just ring fifteen? I thought we were a twelve-hour system, and glad we are, since two times twelve ear-splitting clangs, loud enough to wake the dead, right outside your bloody window in the middle of the night is quite enough entertainment, thank you. (I am reassured that the absence of graves from the churchyard has nothing at all to do with this.)

My curiosity at last getting the better of me (as they used to say in all the better novels) I went to the front door to look, where, lo and behold, there was a shiny white van parked outside the church. A moment or two later, a dapper little man in spotlessly clean coveralls came out, carrying a very smart and shiny tool box. I could tell he was a cut above your average tradesman because his shoes were polished till they shone.

'*Bonjour,*' quoth he.

To which I replied, '*Bonjour* – you fixed the bells?' (I mean I was speaking in French, you know, I'm just trying to make it easier for you.)

'*Bah, oui,* monsieur, they're all working perfectly again,' replied our peripatetic horologist, with the air of a doctor who has just cured a patient of the dreaded lurgy. Or something.

And so they are; the clock bells ring the requisite number of times, one minute before, and on the hour, again. The breakfast, lunch and dinner peals ring out loud and proud over the dreaming, heat-hazy countryside, and life in P'tit Moulin has swung back into its graceful, if unhurried, rhythm. Which means that we can once again be sure when it is time to get up, to go to bed, and most importantly, to pour that nice glass of wine for an *apero*.

I did wonder about the life of that horologist, after we met. What a pleasantly civilised occupation it must be, to travel around the churches and cathedrals of France, most of which are monuments and many, at least around P'tit Moulin, Romanesque. How peaceful to be ensconced in the belfry, able to gaze out over the countryside, with only the doves for company. One would work slowly, respecting the delicacy of the venerable mechanisms one was tasked to tend, gently tightening here and loosening there, oiling a little and cleaning a little, checking and balancing until everything worked – well, like clockwork, I suppose.

And when one was done for the morning, one might repair to one of the excellent cafes or family restaurants that are ever found near French churches. Naturally one would be known, having ministered to the needs of the ticking and tolling mechanisms high above for so long. One might have ongoing conversations with *la patronne* or *le patron*, commenting as their families grew up and spread their wings, then went to live in the cities – which, alas, seems all too often the case in these straitened days when work in the country is so hard to find – except for horologists, tractor mechanics and vets, perhaps.

One would hear how this daughter or that son had met a charming person from the city and now lived there, only returning for holidays. Of grandchildren far away who were but rarely seen and growing up so quickly, doing so well at school...One would note the bitter taint of regret behind the pride and one would understand, listening to the same story again and again as one quartered the country, visiting all the small towns and hearing the same tale: the countryside is dying, monsieur, and nothing can be done. *Bah.*

But equally one might take one's repast outside the great cathedral of some magnificent city, surrounded by all the life and vigour there concentrated, amongst those very same young people who had abandoned the hard old life of the country, and now took their own meals in the busy restaurants. Every cloud has a silver lining, *n'est-ce pas?*

What a lovely view one would have of French life in all its forms, from on high, with the silence to reflect in, and then in the bustling milieu of human life outside. And one would smile, knowing that no matter how depopulated the countryside might become, or how secular the people, no matter how many churches would pass months on end with never a Mass being celebrated in them – or at least, save those commemorating the death of another of the horny-handed – there would always be a demand for church bells and skilled people with clever hands to service the elderly machinery that made them work. A fine life indeed, for the calm of temperament.

All of France's churches actually belong to the State. (We can only presume that the Catholic Church has no funds to maintain them.) Which means that our splendid, chipper and shoe-shined little horologist was actually one of that most highly-envied classes of French professional; he was a *fonctionnaire*, a civil servant. So along with the obvious charm of the job went a nice salary, plenty of holidays, an early retirement, cheap insurance, a 1% mortgage and much, much more, including the opportunity to move to the South for the last five years of his career and retire under the azure sky of the Midi. And guaranteed, for life, since the State is not going to let its monuments fall down. How pleasant indeed.

Hello, there! Six o'clock. Now where did I put that corkscrew?

Spring, Slugs and Spliffs

Spring in France in 2013 was the worst I can remember and summer was not much better. By June I should be on first-name terms with the community of lizards that live in my courtyard, but that year, hardly a hello. They were all still hiding.

Mind you, it was not so bad for all the critters in the yard. My pet hate, *les limaces,* our delightful Burgundian slugs, were positively thriving. I mean, these ones are not shy; they don't even try to hide and they're bright orange anyway. Maybe it's a warning that they taste disgusting. I'll let someone else find out.

The slugs are my enemies because there is historic bad blood between me and their entire accursed class, which dates to when I was much younger.

I was still a teenager, hitch-hiking through Europe. I got picked up by an English trucker, who was a really nice man. He introduced me to *Les Routiers,* where at the time you could get a full meal for 10 francs, or a quid as it was then. (God I'm old.)

I remember him leaning forward on the steering wheel and explaining. 'If you see a place with a *Routiers* sign and a load of lorries outside, you know it'll be good.'

Since at that precise moment I was starving, this was little help and I wondered when lunch was going to happen. Then I saw something and my heart dropped. We were on an arrow-straight stretch of road and ahead of me I could see at least a hundred trucks, big ones, in a queue. I thought we were going to be made to wait while they did Customs or something, but our man was chuckling. 'See?' he said, 'That's gotta be a great place to eat.'

Indeed he was right. Right in the middle of this ruck of trucks was the restaurant, and it was not only vast, more like a barn with a high ceiling where you could see the ancient *charpente,* but also rammed. I've never seen so many truckers in one place. However the service was great and we were soon at one of many long tables with a couple of dozen other truckers, from everywhere it seemed. Lots of them were known to my driver, and it was my first introduction to the strange camaraderie of the road. Truckers are – or at least, they were then – an interesting breed, to say the least.

Anyway, after lunch, we very nearly turned the driver of a Renault

4 into garlic-flavoured raspberry jam. He insisted on his *droit* to enter the main road from the right, immediately in front of our truck belting along at 90 kph – which I wrote about in *French Onion Soup!* However, actual metal-to-metal contact being avoided by the great skill of the driver, we crossed into Italy via the Mont Blanc Tunnel, and dropped down towards Lombardy.

My driver was going to Livorno and I was heading for Venice, so it was time to part, but by that time it was getting dark. He pulled over at the side of the *autostrada* and said 'Passed a couple of Bulgarian trucks a while back, they'll be headed your way. Try throwing a wobbly in front of them.'

Well, I already knew about Bulgarians by repute and anyway I was tired, so I decided not to go the wobbly route and to sleep instead, in what looked like a very nice, dry, concrete spillway at the side of the road. Quite safe and out of sight. So I unpacked my sleeping bag and my mat, and turned in for the night.

I didn't sleep well. All night I itched and scratched. I thought it must have been mosquitoes and covered my head, but it continued. I was so tired, though, that I did nothing more.

I woke in the mistiness of morning, and only then discovered the truth. My pleasant spillway was swarming with slugs and snails, which must have been sliming all over me all night. My clothes, and worse, my exposed skin, even inside my tee-shirt were smeared with the innards of the slugs I had squashed.

It was the biggest dose of the heebie-jeebies I ever had experienced. I actually screamed – I am not given to these demonstrations, you know – and I was shaking like a leaf. I grabbed my stuff, threw it in the rucksack, shouldered it and began to run hell for leather towards Venice – which was still 200 kilometres away. But I was so horrified I couldn't help myself. Alien xenomorphs had nothing on those gastropods.

I was saved from having to leg it all the way to Venice when a venerable Fiat 500 pulled up alongside. It had been tastefully decorated, by hand, with anti-war signs and what I took to be the Italian for Love and Peace in various shades of orange, green and yellow. You must remember that this was in the 1970s.

When it stopped, a strange plume of blue smoke rose through the open sunroof that didn't smell like oil at all. I ran up and sure enough, out hopped the driver, who looked like a better-looking (being Italian) Jerry Garcia clone (you remember him, the *Grateful Dead* guy), with a pretty girl who, for want of better words, was clearly bombed out of her tree. I was bundled into the back, with my rucksack, alongside another two beautiful Italian hippy girls with grins like cats, who were happily smoking joints and giggling.

I wonder if you can imagine what it is like being crammed into the back seat of a *Cinquecento* with that much nubility, smoking some excellent Mary Juana…well, that's for another story. Let's just say that by the time the five of us got to Venice, I had forgotten all about those damn molluscs.

Anyway that is why I really, really can't stand slugs. Makes me shiver still.

However, I have tamed my phobia. Actual physical contact I avoid, but am quite happy to go near enough to the little horrors to fling salt at them. In the courtyard this is spectacularly effective, at the table it improves the garlic-flavoured snot that most restaurants call *escargots* these days. But I really resent what they do to my lettuces and tomatoes. Well, the lettuces they just mow. As soon as they pop their dear little green heads above the soil, that's it, next morning gone.

I thought I'd got smart with the tomatoes and put them in a planter, moving them inside in the evenings and out in the mornings; I took loving care of them. And it was working, you know? Soon I had twenty little tomato plants and I was thinking of all the lovely *salade de tomates a la vinaigrette* – who needs lettuce anyway?

Then one morning there were two missing. I checked. Couldn't see any slugs. The next day, a few more were gone. And the next. When I was down to two poor little blighters, I decided to take drastic action. I took the planter and put it on the garden table, meaning to re-pot the survivors. When I did so there was a loud, and I have to say satisfying crunch, like an eggshell being trodden on.

Underneath the planter, squashed against the table-top, was the biggest *escargot* I've ever seen, outside a restaurant. That's where I like my terrestrial molluscs, by the way, served with garlic butter and washed down with a nice *Sancerre*. Not the ones that taste like rubberised snot; but I know a couple of places where you can get the real thing.

This one seemed very concerned that it had just been rendered homeless. 'Gotcha,' I think is the term.

Now, slugs and snails are not the only fascinating wildlife we are host to here in P'tit Moulin. And no, I am not referring to the natives, for once.

As well as the slugs, the courtyard is usually home to a population of Common Wall Lizards *(Podarcis muralis)*. These are much more pleasant in every way.

They like to hide in the walls, so I built several planters of dry unmortared stone, and am relaxed about the pointing. This gives the wee chaps plenty of places to live and to breed.

I am fond of watching the lizards. Especially on a hot day when they stand on one forefoot and one rear, diagonally opposite, and swap very few seconds. Usually while watching me warily with one yellow eye – of which more, later.

However, the courtyard is sometimes occupied by other reptilian wildlife. The most common is the Grass Snake, which we see many of. They are much more shy than the lizards, though, and they do – as their name suggests – hide in the long grass in what I used to kid myself might one day be a *pelouse* (lawn). Aye, right.

Less welcome are the adders. These are actually as shy as the grass snakes, but they do bite and their venom can be strong enough to kill a dog or even a small child. We have only been invaded twice, and on both occasions by juveniles. They were very carefully caught behind the head (as all the best wildlife shows tell us) swiftly put into a jar and transported several kilometres away. Unlike spiders – and, it turns out, cats – the adders don't seem to come back, so that technique works fine. I am not sure I'd be so confident doing the same with a full-grown one, I have to admit though. That might be a bit too Bear Grylls for me.

We usually have a few frogs, but the population is low. I don't think they like it too much here. Down the road, however, one of the villagers has a proper pond at the bottom of her garden, which for a while was infested with hundreds of frogs. That pond is at least 150 metres away, but they made so much noise that I had to keep the window shut on that side or I would never have slept. Between the frogs and that clock.

It got so bad that her immediate neighbours made a complaint, which didn't go very far. The frogs, argued the frog-woman, were wild animals. She hadn't put them there – which was partially true; she put the spawn there, not the frogs themselves. But neither she nor her neighbours were from the village, so there were no politics to upset if they were ignored. So they were.

Then, when frog-lady was away visiting her sister in Brittany, the neighbours staged a midnight SAS attack. Using torches and a big net they scooped out all the frogs, bundled them into hessian sacks and spirited them away.

I saw the lights but thought nothing of it. This is P'tit Moulin, after all. It's a pretty strange place at times and it does not do to go sticking one's *Anglais* nose into midnight goings-on like that.

The next day I saw Dan, the frog-woman's neighbour – well, one of them – and asked about it. Dan's okay. He told me and I was amazed. There would be hell to pay when she got back.

And there was. She in turn made a complaint and the gendarmes from Nolay came out to investigate the frog-heist. Dan was unworried.

Later he told me that the gendarmes had turned the frog-woman's argument back on her. The frogs were wild; she had already testified that she had not put them there, so no theft was committed, they had reasoned. She countered by insisting that trespass must have occurred, to which our stylish French plod shrugged his shoulders. 'Was your gate locked?'

It hadn't been, of course. So that was that and we all got some sleep again.

By the next spring the frog-woman was no longer the frog-woman; instead, koi carp had taken her fancy. So we were never troubled again by a Biblical plague of frogs.

The koi did not fare well. There are many egrets round here and one soon took up residence. Free fresh fish.

While on the subject of bedroom windows open at night, once, soon after we first arrived, I was downstairs just locking up (I don't bother nowadays) when I heard a scream from the bedroom – where Moira was already ensconced. It was not one of those 'Oh that sounds *really* bad,' screams, so I made my way up in a leisurely manner.

'What's wrong, heart,' quoth I. She was in bed holding the covers up to her nose.

'There's a bloody *bat* in here!'

'Where?' I couldn't see one. Just then a black shape came flittering out of the corridor, whooshed twice round the bedroom and then shot out the door to the spiral staircase behind me, which I had left open.

I was just trying to figure out how I could catch the blighter without harming it, when it flittered back into the bedroom, did another couple of circuits and then whizzed out the open window.

We have owls. There don't seem to be any in my lofts at the moment – they prefer uninhabited buildings. However, my neighbour (you'll meet her) on the western side, only uses her (vast and rambling) house for two months out of every year.

One day she came round. I knew she was on the wheedle.

'There's something in my loft,' says she.

Well, being the local hero that I am, I went to look. In her main loft I found significant amounts of cat droppings. Nice. I pointed out to her that it is hard enough to keep these wretched beasts out of an inhabited house, let alone an unoccupied one. She didn't seem convinced.

'The noise isn't coming from up there,' she said. 'It's coming from further back.'

I went to look. Like a lot of these older houses, hers has a set of lean-tos built onto the original back wall. These tend to be somewhat dark, damp and unpleasant spaces and hers were no different.

'The noise is coming from up there,' she explained.

The lean-to rooms had been fitted with ceilings clad in the cheapest of vee-lining – horrible – and I could tell right away there was a problem. There was obvious, serious damp penetration and the rooms below positively stank.

'That's disgusting,' I said, screwing up my nose.

'Tell me about it,' she replied.

'And it makes a lot of noise, whatever it is?'

'Yes, it's as if the roof's going to come down. Really loud.'

'Well, that ain't cats,' I mused. 'Definitely not.'

She nodded.

'I hope it's not a marten,' I pondered, and I could see she felt the same. My ex-brother-in-law had a marten infestation once. But that tale is for another day.

'All that vee-lining is going to have to come down,' I advised her.

She blanched. 'Really?'

'Well, it's either that or take the roof off,' I explained. 'The vee-lining is right under the rafters. And in any case it's done, look at it.'

She eventually agreed, and as soon as she had departed for Blighty, I got two of the village lads who regularly help me with stuff like that to rip down the vee-lining. Above it was glass wool insulation, in appalling condition, soaking wet and truly disgusting. But in the insulation, there were at least a dozen owls' nests, some old, some apparently under construction. Fortunately it was early spring and there were no eggs or young yet.

Well, that explained the noise. Owls are big birds and while they may be silent in flight, not so on the ground. They had been flying into her main loft and then squeezing through the gap under the tiles into the roof over these lean-tos, where they were well protected. An owl would make plenty of noise doing that.

Now I like owls but they are messy. Their nests are always surrounded by their droppings, and of course, they are meat eaters, so it stinks to high heaven. The neighbour – to make things worse – had a couple of slipped tiles that had been letting water trickle into all this – which was basically a mess of sodden glasswool, prey bones and faeces. And wow did it smell bad.

By the way, that should make you think about glasswool. It's very effective as an insulation, but a whole range of beasties just love it. I remember Calum, once, coming to me to complain about a buzzing in his room. I went to look and could find no problems with the wiring – my first concern being that there might be a fire – so I went up into the loft to investigate. Over the area of his bedroom I spotted a number of bees.

'Ahah,' says I. 'I know what that is.'

That was in the days when we still had a volunteer fire brigade and part of their job was to deal with things like this. So off I went to find the deputy mayor. Sure enough, later that day they arrived, with a small, grey-bearded man. It turned out he was an apiculturist.

'They'll be in the insulation,' he said. 'They love it. Nice and warm.'

Sure enough, using smoke to make the bees drowsy, he and the firemen soon had cut out a section about a metre square of insulation and carefully placed in sacks. The way they did it. using shovels to undercut the hive and lift it clear, suggested to me that perhaps they had done this before.

They showed what they had found: the lower half of the insulation, which was 25 centimetres deep, had been turned into a beehive.

'I'll give them a home,' said the beekeeper, reassuringly. And he did; he even brought me a pot of honey.

Bees are not the only insect to watch out for, and at least bees are useful. The other day, though, I was standing outside the house next to my car, chatting to one of my friends who had happened to pass by. He was going for a cycle ride. Suddenly I felt a sting on my back, and then another. On the third, I turned and looked – there seemed to be a lot of wasps around.

'Look,' said my friend. 'They're coming from your car door.'

It was clear that they were flying in and out of the gap between the door and the front wing. They were being extremely aggressive, even for wasps and I thought, 'Uh-oh, something's up.'

I bade my friend farewell and gingerly opened the door to have a look. There was a complete nest built in the door jamb, and the wasps were aggressively defending it.

I had used the car only the evening before, to go and buy beer. Fast workers. Anyway I went and fetched a nice long pole and flicked the nest onto the road, then hopped in the car and took off before they realised it was me.

So be careful, hm?

Another beastie that we often find lurking in the dark recesses of our dream homes here in *la France profonde,* is the *loir* – a dormouse. Now this is not actually a mouse at all, though it is a rodent. They are incredibly cute little things but, once again, they make a terrible mess and their nests stink.

They are also subject to sudden death as a result of shock. (I'm not kidding.) One afternoon we were out in the courtyard having lunch *en famille.* Unusually, the table was next to the back wall of the house – I can't remember why. We were all laughing and joking, as we usually did, when suddenly there was a light thump and a very recently dead dormouse fell on the table.

As you might imagine, there was something of a reaction. This ranged from one of Moira's screams, to expressions of horror on the part of the boys. Cait just stared.

By that time there was Internet, so I looked it up. Somewhere in the roof there must have been a dormouse nest and this one had wandered. Our revelry had scared it and it dropped dead from heart failure. Apparently.

That's what it said on the Interwebs, so it must be true.

P'tit Moulin Chicken

Calum had loved our new home from the start, as had I. It was a wreck, it was indescribably filthy, it had no hot water and I have never in my life seen décor that was more offensive, but it just exuded charm. And now we two lads were to be there together to do some serious male bonding while Moira was locked up in the clutches of the Maternity Service at the Big Blue Hospital in Beaune.

As readers of the first book may recall, Moira had begun her contractions two weeks prematurely, probably due to having damaged her placenta while knocking down a concrete pillar. It stopped the sun getting to her favoured spot in the courtyard. Well, *I* didn't make her do it. What do you think I am, an ogre?

We had, somewhat fortunately, stocked up on food the day before the emergency so at least there were provisions to spare. I have always been a capable cook; my mother took the view that men who can't look after themselves are an affront to womankind and insisted that her sons knew the basics of Home Economics. This may have had something to do with her own revulsion for domestic chores, but it had the desired result. I wondered what we should eat. Yes, I thought, chicken would fill the bill. Chicken and – ha, what have we here? – Couscous. Couscous it would be.

The first issue was roasting it. The house had come with a gas range that looked like it had been made by the same lads as built the Eiffel Tower. It was massive, squat, rusty and extremely ugly. And it was the most filthy object I have ever been that close to. I've seen the underside of cars I would sooner eat from. In fact it was so filthy that Moira had refused to even consider using it and had instead insisted on using the stove in our caravan and bringing the cooked meals down from the field in a barrow. Just what the ever-observant neighbours thought of this I never discovered.

I, however, was not to be derailed in my plan. Tonight's meal would be cooked in the house, and that was that. The cooker – which I soon christened 'The Beast' (the first of several) came apart easily enough, but cleaning it was more of an issue.

We still had no plumbed hot water supply and I had just dismantled the only means of heating same into a pile of extremely greasy scrap metal. I was almost on the point of succumbing to using the caravan after all (it's funny how principle can fly out the window when confronted with a cooker that hasn't been cleaned in several decades,) but I was made of sterner stuff, I told myself. Had I not seen an oil stove in the garage?

Yes indeed I had, and after twenty minutes or so I even managed to find it. And a little while later I found some oil to put in it.

Now I was all set and I put a large pan to boil while I continued disembowelling the beast. Detergent and hot water would soon shift that grease, I reasoned, and I was right, though my initial estimate of how much of each would be needed was woefully short of the mark. But after an hour or son's scrubbing and washing, using huge quantities of water heated on the little oil stove, which itself looked as if it had not seen action since La Guerre, I had a stack of clean bits that could be reassembled.

By the time I got the beast back together the shadows were already lengthening and both Calum and I were definitely Very Hungry Indeed. Gingerly did I attach the gas bottle and attempt the ceremonial first lighting of one of the top burners. I struck the fateful match and opened the tap. To my amazement, and to Callus's I think – he had been watching this part of the process carefully from a safe distance – it lit and I did not immediately lose what my activities as a plumber had left of my eyebrows. In fact, all the burners and the oven worked perfectly and The Beast, although no less hideous than before, was at last clean and smelling sweet.

But it was by then near eight, the evening was transforming into night, and we still had to cook our celebrated chicken. I wondered if this sort of thing explained the French inability to eat dinner before ten o'clock at night. Necessity, you know, is the Mother of Invention, and I was determined to have a roast chicken before it got dark. How was I to prepare it?

So far, all I had found was the chook, the couscous and some herbs; it seemed a little commonplace for such a grand occasion. Suddenly an idea flashed into mind. There was a plum tree in the courtyard, its branches laden to the point of almost breaking with fruit. Calum had been staving off the hunger by lightening its load. I lit the oven and left it to pre-heat – A Great Invention was indeed about to be made!

Calum and I gathered a few handfuls of plums, and I stoned them. Into a greased dish they went, along with some garlic, and then our chicken on top. Upon her plump firm breasts did I smear the greatest of the Burgundian magic ingredients, Dijon mustard. But to my horror I saw that there was too little, and stared disaster in the face. But on looking around I saw a jar of *Bonne Maman* jam (we were still buying the expensive stuff then.)

Well, Dijon mustard comes in a jar, and so does jam, I reasoned, so on it went. It certainly looked entertaining, and Calum approved. A decent slosh of red wine into the dish along with a couple of cloves of garlic and some herbs, some foil over the top and into the oven, which was already belting out some serious heat, it went.

The thing to do, I reckoned, was to incinerate the little bugger at the highest temperature possible. This would, I hoped, caramelise the jam and make the skin lovely and crispy – my, I'm getting hungry writing this, I don't know about you – and at the same time, with any luck, get us lads fed before midnight.

Thus was created a new culinary delicacy, *Roast Chicken with Plums and Jam*. I like to think it has a rather Epicurean smack to it. You know, all lying around on couches enjoying the *pullo* and whatever jam is in Latin (I forget; my classical education was a long time ago) and looking forward to the orgy later. Well, there was always an orgy after dinner, wasn't there?

That we were present at a great moment in comestible history became more and more obvious as an aroma, at once sweet and richly savoury, began to fill the kitchen, so that we soon became weak with hunger and the desire to eat. Our mouths watered, our bellies rumbled and I found ridiculous things to do to divert us until the moment of Revelation. At last I pronounced our repast ready and turned off the oven while I prepared the couscous.

Calum and I sat out in the courtyard at an ancient rickety table and tucked in. How tasty was that humble supermarket chook! The meat tender, the gravy toothsome, the skin crisped to a treat. It was wonderful, and, the edge taken off my searing hunger, I sipped a glass or two of rough table wine and began to relax, as we watched the stars come out and gasped as the bats flitted around the old buildings with seemingly magical agility.

I was blissfully, almost beatifically happy; and so was Calum, who perhaps had not seen me so relaxed in a long time, and now snuggled sleepily into my side sucking his thumb and looking up at the P'tit Moulin bats dancing and flitting below stars set in a firmament of deep indigo.

Croutons and Cheese!

There we were, sated from our repast, safe in our Dream Home in France. What a happy pair of Moulinards were we!

Wine and Such

Pete (the hang-dog) and Sharon (the basket-case) were an *Anglais* couple (real *Anglais,* not Scottish ones) who lived in the village, but the fact that we regarded them as being quite a lot odd should not disguise the truth: they were a big help to us in our early months. To describe us as 'painfully naïve' would be an understatement.

Pete had been great with his advice about the *affouage* (which readers of the first book will know all about and so may nod wisely at this point) and even if his advice tended to be handed out in the style of the computer in *Hitchhiker's Guide to the Galaxy,* a fair bit was actually true, you know.

I had been, for some time, curious about the signs outside *caves* – wine shops – that said *'Vin en VRAC'* and had asked Jacques, my friend from Nuits St Georges, about this. His habitually laconic reply had been that it meant the *cave* sold in wholesale, and I had assumed this translated as 'vast quantities for resale.' Pete was the one who set me straight. Oh no, he explained, they'll sell you as little as five litres. All you need is a *bidon.* A *bidon*, it turned out, was a jerry-can.

What you did was take your jerry-can to the *cave* and they would fill it, and then charge you the wholesale litre price, which in 1993, varied between 3 francs to 6 francs depending on where you went, how much you bought, and just how rough you could stand your tipple. Our local *cave* sold a very pleasant local table wine, 12 degrees, for 5 francs a litre, and this was what we had been enjoying, and even commenting on, at Pete's table.

To give you an idea of what that means, in those halcyon pre-Euro days, a franc equated, more or less, to ten pence, or ten francs to £1. So our excellent wine was costing us about thirty-eight pence a bottle. I have this right here in my notebook.

Even today – and I just checked – the price is 1.20 Euros per litre, or £1.00 GBP, more or less.

Anyone used to the egregiously offensive level of duty applied to wine in Britain will probably be shocked by these prices, or, if you happen to be in France, delighted, as I was. Needless to say our table was always provided with adequate quantities of excellent wine.

In later years, during times when I was not resident in France, I was able to travel to our P'tit Moulin Dream Home and have holidays there twice a year and it did not cost a penny, because of this discrepancy in prices. Why?

Well, as a UK citizen, I was allowed to bring back as much wine for personal consumption as I wished, from France, without paying any duty; I couldn't legally sell it, though I could give as much as I wanted away.

Moira and I consumed a bottle of wine a night between us, let us say eight bottles per week. In six months we would therefore need to buy 26x8 = 208 bottles of wine. Add a few parties, that sort of thing, and allow that in six months, 250 bottles of wine are required for two people to live in harmony. Now thanks to the officially-sanctioned thievery enacted by the British State, in those days a bottle of wine, that could actually be drunk, in the UK, cost £3.50, and I'm being conservative, very. Yet at that time, *cave* wine on *VRAC* cost about 80p a bottle. If we brought back 180 litres from France, which is the UK Customs 'guideline' for two people, (and it is only a guideline, not a legal limit,) then that equated to just over 250 bottles, which would cost £200.

However if I bought 250 bottles in the UK it would have cost me £875 at minimum, and it would not have been very good wine. Therefore I saved £675 by buying my wine in France, which was more than enough to drive to Burgundy and back and also cover the ferry. Indeed it would even allow some spending money when I was there and I got to enjoy good French table wine when I came home.

And by the way, I lived in Scotland. For you English the deal is even better and you would be fools not to take advantage of it. Which also makes your recent decision to permanently put an end to such delights appear even more spectacularly dense than it did at first glance.

So you see, dear reader, I am indebted to the ineffably morose Pete. I had two holidays in France a year and it cost me absolutely nothing, or at least, no more than I would have spent anyway.

And best of it is, there is nothing that any creep in the Customs service, any jobsworth in the Treasury, or even any overpaid Minister of State can do about it. It's all perfectly legal and one of the benefits of being a European. Indeed, when HM Customs tried to get a bit heavy handed and suggest that the voluntary guidelines for what an individual could bring in were actually legal limits, the European Commission quickly stepped in and stopped them. Ho ho ho. It does make the wine taste just that little bit sweeter when you know every sip is putting one over on the Chancellor of the Exchequer and his goon squad.

Eye Trouble

They say good health is the greatest of gifts, and as you get older, the more truth you see in the old saw.

One Saturday morning Moira came to me. She was obviously concerned, in that way that she has when she's been worrying about something for a while and has at last decided to spill the beans.

'What's wrong?' I asked.

'I seem to have gone blind in the corner of one eye,' she replied.

That brought me up short. 'Has anything happened?'

'Well, I smashed my head off the low lintel on the kitchen door the other day.' (The same one I had encountered at the time of the sledgehammer incident, described in the first book; I hadn't yet got round to fitting a new one.) 'I think I damaged myself.'

As it happens, I have some training in First Aid, so I sat her down and had a look at her eyes. There was nothing obviously wrong, so I decided to do a pupil dilation test to see if there was a bit of concussion from the knock. Gently I put my hand over her eyes to shut out the light and held it there for thirty seconds or so.

When I took it away and looked again I got the shock of my life. Her right eye was behaving quite normally. It was looking anxiously at me and the iris, from dilated, had closed nicely. But not only was her left eye still widely dilated, it was also gazing serenely out the window.

That was one of the biggest frights I've ever had. I immediately got on the phone to the local doctor, who agreed to see her right away. We bundled into the car and scooted down to Nolay, where the GP performed a similar test and shook his head. 'You'll have to see an ophthalmologist,' he said. 'This is more than I can deal with.'

Now if you're used to the NHS in Blighty, you would assume, as I did, that, especially since it was Saturday morning, we would get a little note, and perhaps an appointment in a couple of weeks. But not a bit of it. The local doctor got on the phone and there was a brief exchange in rapid French; after which he put the phone down and looked gravely at the crazy foreigners.

'There is an opthalmologist at Beaune. She is due to finish her surgery in half an hour, but she'll wait for you.' He scribbled a few lines into Moira's *Carnet de Santé*, the little notebook that everyone in France carried back then with their medical history, and then proceeded to draw out a plan. In a matter of minutes we were on the familiar road to Beaune, more than a little worried, by now.

Doctor Baillet was as good as her word and had kept her clinic open, for which I thanked her; She quickly corrected me, saying that she was the duty opthalmo in the area, and if necessary she would have opened up for Moira anyway. Soon she was minutely examining the interior of Moira's eyes with highly-impressive looking optical devices. After about fifteen minutes, she excused herself and left the room, leaving us, Moira, Calum, Sandy and me, in apprehensive silence.

The doctor came back in after a short time, sat down again and turned to us. 'You clearly have an area of your left eye which has become blind,' she said to Moira, in English. 'But I can't see any physical damage to the retina at all. It's quite intact, not detached or torn. So we have to check for neural damage, and I have arranged for you to see a Consultant Neurologist in Dijon.'

'When?'

'Tomorrow,' she replied, a little apologetically. 'His surgery is closed now and he has other engagements this afternoon. But he will open up for you tomorrow. Could you be there for eleven?'

Naturally we could, though we were still sufficiently naïve not to realise that we could simply have arranged an ambulance and had it reimbursed thanks to our lovely Form E111. What was perhaps most surprising about the exchange was that the ophthalmologist was genuinely apologetic that the neurologist could not see Moira the same day.

As it happened, my mother had only the previous year had a fall that had resulted in part of one of her retinas becoming detached; it took the NHS three months to arrange an appointment with an ophthalmologist, by which time the damage was permanent. Lord knows how long she'd have had to wait to see a neurologist. Yet in France we had seen an opthalmologist less than two hours after our first call to the GP, and she was embarrassed that her colleague could not see Moira right away. The difference between the two systems was simply staggering.

I remember a story appearing in the early 90s when one of the Scottish Health Boards caused a furore by going £6 million over budget; then, that was enough to raise an eyebrow. Less widely publicised, but nevertheless equally true, was that the same Health Board had over sixty non-clinical senior managers being paid over £100,000 each; then, that was enough to raise both eyebrows. As ever, the multiplicity of layers of bureaucracy that is apparently necessary for the first thing to happen in any British organisation had broken the very budget it was supposed to maintain.

One did have to ask if the NHS was being run for the benefit of patients or the benefit of management, and the answer, to me at least, was quite obvious. Patients are a necessary evil; everything would run so much more smoothly if they were not there to gum the system up. In France, the system is, very obviously, designed to put patient care first. The argument is not about the quality of the individual doctors or nurses; it's about the way the systems are structured. One system is designed to help doctors help patients and the other is designed to make managers' lives easy.

The next day, Moira and I, along with Calum, Sandy and Dee – who would have wrecked the house had we left her – made our way to Dijon. It is a lovely city and the road, along the Vallée de l'Ouche, is one of the most beautiful I know anywhere; but somehow we never noticed the delights of the scenery or the charms of the ancient and historic city, that morning. We were very worried people; Moira's sight had become markedly worse overnight and now she was quite blind in about half the visual field of her left eye. To make matters worse an intense headache had set in.

The neurologist was a dapper, small man, with thick black hair and black-framed glasses. He carried out a series of tests on Moira, walking a straight line with her eyes closed and then open, touching her nose with one finger and so on. My wife's sheer inability to perform any of these simple tasks would have been hilarious if the cause had been the demon drink – that it was not made the whole thing terrifying. Something was clearly not right inside that beautiful head. At the end of the consultation, which took about twenty minutes, the neurologist sat down and indicated that we should do the same.

'We will have to do a full set of tests,' he said. 'Clearly there is something wrong. I am going to book your wife into Beaune Hospital tomorrow and will ask for everything they can do – X-Rays, CT scan, bloods, lumbar puncture. This will give us a great deal more information.'

He paused, looked at the notes he had made, and then looked up at us again, earnestly. 'I am afraid that you should prepare yourselves; in my opinion the tests will only confirm that the cause of the problem is *sclérose en plaques*; multiple sclerosis. It is, I am afraid, not uncommon in women who have children in their thirties.'

I had only ever heard of this scourge and was unprepared. 'What does that mean – can it be treated?'

'Monsieur, there are two forms, aggressive and chronic. If the latter, then much can be done to control the effects of the disease and there is no reason why Madame should not have a long life, perhaps with some restrictions; if the former...' He spread his fingers. 'Then there are still things that we can do. The tests they will carry out at Beaune should help confirm what we are dealing with. In the meantime, after her tests, I propose to treat your wife with very high doses of steroids, which should arrest the progress of the disease.'

In the modern world, there is no question that the very first thing I should have done on returning to the house – in a state of shock, as we all were – would have been to get on the Internet and do some serious research. But there was no Internet then, and there was no library in P'tit Moulin. So we were completely in the dark. All we knew was that Moira was going to have to go into hospital, and we did not know what the result would be.

It being Sunday night, Moira's father John phoned from Surrey. It was impossible not to let him know what was going on and his response was predictably reassuring – 'We'll be with you later in the week.' I was reluctant to trouble Moira's parents in this way but they would never have forgiven me if I had not told them, and the situation had turned out badly.

The next morning – still not having learned about the ambulances – I drove Moira down to the Big Blue Hospital at Beaune and checked her in. Overnight, her condition had deteriorated again and it was clear that she was having trouble keeping balance, so I found a wheelchair and, despite her protestations, put her in it with Sandy on her lap while we headed for the neurology ward.

On the way we bumped into Christine, the lovely, if shambolic midwife I mentioned in *French Onion Soup!* In her usual style she came to our aid and brought warmth and reassurance, not in the form of glib platitudes but in genuine sympathy and solidarity. I can think of no other words. This was a woman who knew pain intimately – who must have suffered agonies every single day of her life, due to her body having been wrecked in a near-fatal car accident. Yet she could still give of herself to two frightened, lonely individuals who were beginning to feel a very long way from home. Hers is not a face I will ever forget, nor her kindness.

Then began a whirlwind of activity for Moira and I was politely asked to let her rest as the tests would continue that afternoon; so I meandered my way back up to our eyrie in the Arrière-côte and set to maintaining a sensible domestic routine. One thing was for sure – there was no way I was going to get any work done until the results came.

John and Sandra arrived on the Tuesday afternoon and we went to see Moira together. She was a little sedated, having just had a lumbar puncture, which she said was the most horrifically painful thing she had ever experienced. It even beat childbirth, she said. All the other tests had been carried out, too.

The neurologist from Dijon arrived while we were there and immediately took control of the situation, examining the test results as he stood by Moira's bed with a small bevy of junior doctors and nurses surrounding him. They seemed almost in awe. At length, he put down the charts and nodded. 'We will begin the steroid treatment tomorrow,' he said with finality.

'Are you sure?' I asked. 'Do you know which form it is yet?'

'No. But your wife's condition is still getting worse and it is imperative that we act quickly. The treatment will begin tomorrow.'

Not for the first time a feeling of terrified helplessness in front of the undeniably efficient French health service washed over me. I suppose at least in Britain we'd have had weeks, or more likely months, to prepare ourselves; here it was a struggle just to keep up with the pace the doctors moved at. Bear in mind, this was less than four days since Moira had first complained of her condition. She'd have been lucky to have got a GP appointment in that time at home.

There was little to talk about at dinner that night; we were all worried sick. Sandra had been a nurse and she realised that the levels of steroid dosage that he was proposing to give Moira were so dramatic that the neurologist must have been very worried.

We had agreed that we would not visit her until the evening the next day, after the steroid treatment was done with; I was a little surprised, then, when she called the house at around eleven. 'They're not doing any treatment.'

'What?'

'They're not doing any treatment. They say I can come home soon.'

Frankly it didn't make any more sense than the first time. 'Why not?'

'Well, there's another neurologist here. Apparently he's in charge, not the guy from Dijon. He's been off for a few days and this is the first time he's had a chance to see the results. And he says we have to wait. I think. They won't talk to me in English.'

'I'm coming down.'

I think that old Granada could have driven the road itself by the time I was done; anyway I left John and Sandra in charge of the boys and scooted down. Monsieur *le docteur* Berthauld could not come right away, but he knew I was waiting and would see me as soon as he had finished his rounds.

His words, when I saw him, were confusing. I asked why they were not doing the steroid treatment and he said there was no need. This surprised me, but he carried on; the steroid treatment was very aggressive, with the possibility of serious side-effects and he was not about to sanction it if it were not absolutely necessary.

'So you don't think it's *sclérose en plaques*?'

'Oh yes, I believe it certainly is.'

'But then…that's what the other neurologist said, and that we had no choice but to use the steroids.'

'No, monsieur; the steroids only arrest the condition, and furthermore the patient is under *my* care, in *my* hospital. The decision is mine. Not his.'

'But?'

'Your wife's condition has stabilised. In fact it has improved somewhat, with the area of affected vision reduced.'

I tell you, they might have the most efficient health service on the planet, but man those French doctors have a weird way of breaking the good news.

'So?'

'So, we won't be giving her possibly dangerous treatment to do something that has already happened. If she continues to improve we can let your wife come home on Friday, I think.'

'And that's it?'

'Oh no, monsieur. I am confident that this is not the aggressive form of *sclérose en plaques*; the pathology, of rapid deterioration and then partial recovery, is typical of the chronic form. So your wife will be on medication for the rest of her life; just not steroids, today anyway. I am going to arrange that she has an MRI (*IRM* in French, typically) and that should let us know exactly what we are dealing with. Meantime we just have to make her comfortable.' He paused, for the first time during the interview showed some sympathy, and almost smiled. 'I will give you some material to read on *sclérose en plaques*; you're going to need it.'

I wondered about the neurologist's attitude; he was by far the least friendly professional I had met within the French health service. I think it was partly just his manner, but Moira told me later that the neurologist from Dijon had been at Beaune that morning to begin the steroid treatment. The two men had had a very firm and frank exchange of views, which Moira had not understood, but I think I had the gist of; a territorial dispute with her at the centre. A senior consultant pissing contest, in other words. However the cool logic of the 'wait-and-see' approach was at least more reassuring and anyway, there was nothing we could do other than go along with the clinicians' decisions.

Moira was released back into my care on the Friday. Now that should not be taken to mean that she was better; she was just not as bad. In the first place she simply could not remain upright for more than about twenty minutes, so she was confined to bed. Her skin, she said, was constantly prickling and tingling all over, as if she had pins and needles everywhere. It must have been torture. She had a blinding headache and although vision had returned to her left eye, she still could not focus properly with it, making reading impossible. Finally, she couldn't stand bright lights.

The hospital had sent her home with a package of various medicines, which basically were designed to control her pain, and the local GP was booked to drop by on a daily basis for the first week. Meanwhile our bedroom became the hub for the house. John and Sandra stayed until the beginning of the following week and then, seeing that Moira was at least stable and in good hands, left us to it.

And then, two Saturdays after she had first told me of her problem, Moira got up and said, 'It's gone.'

'What's gone?'

'Everything – the *sclérose* – whatever – it's gone. Like it was never there.' She was standing with her robe on by the window focussing on the steeple clock, covering first one eye, and then the other. 'Perfect.'

'Yes, but can you touch your nose with your finger with your eyes shut?'

She turned, grinned, and did exactly that. Then put her tongue out. 'See?'

I made to get up but she moved more quickly, and slipped off her robe. 'Not so fast. I want to be sure it's all better.'

That, however, was not the end of it; two weeks later Moira was laid low with headaches, loss of balance, and prickly skin again. The GP came in response to my call, and sat on the bed, clucking his tongue. 'That's typical of the *sclérose*,' he said, in a morbidly cheerful manner. 'It comes, it goes.'

This did not cheer Moira one bit; but sure enough, a few days later, it went.

She was due to have her MRI the next week and so we made our way to Dijon, fully expecting the worst, and the boys and I amused ourselves in the ante-room while we listened to the pounding boom-boom of the machine as Moira's magnetic particles were excited. The radiographer was very sweet and showed us the images of her brain afterwards. They're like that in France; they don't get all funny about people asking to see for themselves what's wrong with them.

'Is it…*sclérose en plaques*?' I asked, hesitating to confirm the truth that we had all by then come to accept.

The doctor laughed. 'No. See – no *plaques*. No *plaques*, no *sclérose*. Frankly, I would be amazed if this were *sclérose en plaques*. There's just no evidence.'

'So what is it?'

'I don't know. Possibly a virus. Possibly stress.'

'Stress?'

'Maybe. I'm a radiologist, not a neurologist, monsieur. All I can tell you is, there are no *plaques* on your wife's *scléra*.' He shrugged.

There were to be more consequences of whatever it was that had affected Moira, but at no time in the next fifteen years did she ever suffer another attack of the mysterious disease that had so frightened us. Mark you, on a routine visit to the GP, eight years after the event, he asked her if the *sclérose en plaques* had ever come back. Moira – with some relief – told him it had not; it was gone.

Croutons and Cheese!

'For the time being,' he said, knowingly.

The Drains

In the mid-nineties a great scourge came to darken the skies over villages and towns the length and breadth of Europe. In P'tit Moulin, of course, this was dealt with in the usual idiosyncratic style.

For hundreds – nay, thousands – of years, the loyal Moulinards had been fertilising the soil in the natural way. When they needed to pass on what was already a part of them, they went out to the vegetable patch and relieved themselves there. Simple, convenient, and sustainable.

Modernity seems to have caught up a few hundred years ago with the invention of the 'commode.' This was what the English call a 'chamber-pot,' and we Scots call a 'chanty.' That's with a 'ch,' like chicken. In the fashionable parts of France, elegant ceramic bowls made it possible for the citizenry to relieve themselves without wandering up to the vegetable patch in the middle of the night. A century later or so, the stalwart folk of rural Burgundy decided that they too would adopt the new system. It doesn't do to rush these things. But a ceramic chanty was really a bit too effete for the sons and daughters of the soil and the weapon of choice was instead a bucket, which fitted into a wooden chair with a hole cut in the seat.

By the 1960s, this system had reached breathtaking heights of sophistication and luxury, with plastic buckets with specially rolled-over top lips that did not cut into the user's backside and – oh revelation – fitted lids. These kept the contents from stinking the place out until the rain stopped long enough to go out and spread them on the tomatoes.

That this system was still in use until recently was proved beyond doubt when we discovered several such buckets, replete with contents, in the darker parts of our new dream home; but perhaps we shall not go into that right now.

For the rest of rural France, sometime in the sixties, flush sanitation became all the rage. Now the thing is that the old system, while shocking to we moderns, was practical and sustainable. There was plenty farmland to be fertilised and not that many people. The doings were recovered by Mother Earth and put to good use.

That all changed with the arrival of the flush water closet, for now all that beneficial manure was simply washed away, down the drain and into – the nearest river or lake. It was really a terrible waste, but it was the price of modernity. At least the fish were well-fed.

All went along just fine until that terrible cloud I mentioned began to form in the north. That this was a cloud partly of French making was neither succour nor solace. Across the whole of France did it spread its shadow, and I do not doubt the rest of Europe too.

A European Directive made it illegal to discharge raw sewage into the environment. And 'the environment' included rivers and lakes. Oh definitely.

Coincidentally, the same Directive made the discharge of sewage into inshore water also illegal, and resulted in what appeared to be the entire coastline of Britain being turned on its ear by huge mechanical diggers, but that was not a concern to the Moulinards, who were some 400 miles from the sea.

Being a journalist I was aware of this new and exciting development and I have to say I did not think it was too bad an idea; after all, Calum did like to play in the river, and since we had discovered that it doubled as the village sewer, we had stopped him. At the same time I was somewhat concerned, as we ourselves had no septic tank, nor did we have anywhere we could put one – and this was something we had in common with most of the rest of the village.

There is a large, man-made lake at the chateau, which is at the lowest end of the village, which appeared to be used mainly as a duck-pond. Certainly I never saw anyone swimming in it; and the muddy water, like thick pea soup, which always had a light covering of frothy scum, was as seriously uninviting as any water I have ever seen. Since the little river ran into this, and then out again, perhaps it is not quite true to say that P'tit Moulin did not have a sewage treatment facility – at least it did appear to have a very large settling tank. And the ducks seemed to grow very fat and healthy on it.

Anyway, I was not surprised to see a message on the Municipal Notice Board, saying that there was to be a Town Meeting on the subject of 'Sanitation.'

I explained to Moira that I would have to attend, as I had no idea what was proposed in the matter of resolving the village's sanitation problem and I felt that I should find out.

So, on the appointed night, I put on my smart journalist clothes and walked the twenty-five yards from our front door to the *Mairie*.

I patiently waited on one of the long benches which had, as usual on these occasions, been pressed into service as seating. Little by little, the benches were occcupied by the blue-denimed posteriors of the horny handed sons of P'tit Moulin. Grunts of suitably masculine recognition and welcome were exchanged; there was not a woman in the place. I was aware of a fairly powerful aroma of alcohol. filing the air. Almost made my eyes water. A murmuration of chat began to mount.

A man whom I recognised and later came to know as Monsieur Bardeau entered. He was, to put it very mildly, steamboats. (A term, by the way, that originated in the Glaswegian tradition of taking a trip on a Clyde steamer on Sunday, not for the bracing air, but because you could buy drink at sea and all the pubs on dry land were shut, it being the Sabbath. These days you don't have to put anything like as much effort into getting pissed.)

Anyway I knew Monsieur Bardeau was one of the floating population of men who could normally be found in the cafe and I had seen him the worse for wear before; but this time he really was, without being too blunt, completely rat-arsed.

He spotted me, came straight up and barked something out in French. You have to remember that the vagaries of the Moulinard *patois* were still a mystery to me and largely remain so; but I gathered that he wanted to know why I was there. I replied, as best I could, that I lived across the road. His reply surprised me.

'I know, I know – but why are you here?' He was being quite aggressive and while I was not intimidated – he looked as if he might fall over at any moment – I was perplexed at why he was so upset. I made a valiant attempt to explain that as a house-owner in the village I had a right to know what was being proposed as a solution to the drainage problem.

At least I think that's what I said – whatever, it didn't help. The good M. Bardeau was even more incensed by my response and his face suffused a deep, and alarming, shade of purple.

'*Mais non! C'est pas possible,*' he began, but was cut off – and I was saved further assault of garlic and *caporal* – by the mayor, who arrived at that point and led M. Bardeau, gently but firmly, to a seat on the other side of the room, quietly murmuring something in his ear. It seemed to mollify him and the threat of immediate attack receded somewhat. I was aware, however, that others on that side of the room were staring at me with a not altogether friendly curiosity; and at the same time, people I did not know from Adam, on my side of the room, were giving me a cheery display of the shortcomings of French rural dentistry.

It felt like the two sides of a kirk at a shotgun wedding but I had no time to reflect on what this might mean, as the mayor called the meeting to order. Doubtless he was aware that things might get unruly if a firm grip were not kept on the reins; the smell of alcohol was pretty strong and it looked as though Angèle had been having a busy night.

The mayor took a seat at the table set on the podium at the end of the room and rapped his gavel on the table. He began by welcoming everyone to the evening's discussions and after a moment or so of explanation, paused and looked around the room meaningfully.

No sooner had he done so than M. Bardeau stood up again, stabbed his finger at me and demanded, 'Why is *he* here?' I could not help but notice that this was accompanied by a somewhat querulous rumble from a group of people sitting near to my unsuspected nemesis, whom I could now see bore a more than passing resemblance to his good person; from which I deduced that this was his family. I began to wonder amongst whose family I might have found myself.

I could see this was wearing a bit thin with the mayor. I doubt very much if he wanted me there, but he knew he could not eject me, no matter how much it might have pleased Bardeau. He explained that this was a public meeting and that as a householder and taxpayer in the commune I had every right to attend. I was reassured by a rather more approving rumble from my side of the room; M. Bardeau sat down, having apparently conceded the point.

Then the mayor continued on to the main subject of the meeting.

'We are here,' he intoned gravely, 'Because we have had an official complaint from the *Departement's* Bureau of Sanitation.' He looked around the hall gravely, as if to emphasise the severity of the issue.

'The matter, which I am sure you are all aware of, concerns Monsieur Rey, who is not with us tonight. M. Rey, as you will doubtless remember, believes that effluent from M. Bardeau's, er, farm, is polluting his land and in particular, fouling his cattle.'

M. Bardeau leapt to his feet. *'Toujours la meme histoire! C'est absolument absurde!'* he yelled, but the mayor waved him down and his allies dragged him back to his seat.

Another voice, from his side of the room, piped up. 'It's ridiculous that Rey should go to the *Departement*. He should have come to the Town Council!'

The mayor's face displayed the resignation of a man well used to this ruse. He stood up.

'Now,' he said, moving to an enormous tome that had been laid out at the end of the table. Several paper markers had been inserted in the pages, and he opened it at the first. 'In 1978, M. Rey complained to the Town Council about this, stating that every winter when his field flooded, his cows became fouled with,' he looked around the assembly, 'Human faeces. And the Town Council decided to do nothing.'

Again, he looked around meaningfully. 'In 1983, M. Rey complained again and this time the Town Council decided to examine the matter in person.' He looked up. 'The letter of complaint, for reasons that were never clear, was dealt with in the summer, and, if you recall, we all went to look at M. Rey's cattle. But the problem, apparently, only occurs in the winter.' He shrugged. 'So there was no evidence.'

He turned to another page. 'In 1988, M. Rey wrote to the Town Council again and insisted that if action were not taken to prevent effluent polluting his field, he would make a complaint to the *Departement*. It would appear from this letter that he believes that someone had held up the delivery of the previous one,' the mayor held up the offending epistle, 'So that it would arrive at the wrong time of year. The Town Council was annoyed by this suggestion, which was, of course, surely unfounded, and as a result voted to take no action. And now, in 1993,' he said, closing the book. 'M. Rey has indeed gone to the *Departement*, so the Bureau of Sanitation is involved.'

The mayor shrugged. 'I think M. Rey feels he has been waiting long enough.'

Croutons and Cheese!

'But the Bureau of Sanitation?' came another voice, and the mayor nodded. This was indeed a truly grave matter, I could see by the mayor's demeanour, and he turned his gaze around the gathering. 'I am obliged, as mayor, to assist the Bureau in their investigations.' He shrugged. 'If we can't come to a solution tonight, the Bureau will take matters into their own hands.'

He returned to his seat. 'The problem, as you are all aware, is that M. Bardeau's drains go into the little stream at the back of his house. This passes through M Rey's field and then through a culvert under the road before it joins the river. Unfortunately, in winter, there is so much water that M. Rey's field floods, and his cows are soon up to their knees in M. Bardeau's shit.'

He shrugged and held his hands up, making a Gallic pout, as if to say, 'It's not *my* shit, you know.'

At this M. Bardeau could take it no longer. 'This is an outrage! My family is from P'tit Moulin! We are not some stuck-up incomers. The farm has been ours for hundreds of years! All my life I shat in that stream. My father shat in it. My grandfather shat in it! We *always* shat in it! What's the problem? Rey's father knew we shat there when he bought his farm. Stuff him!' He swore. 'And what about the people who live upstream from me? Isn't their shit involved? Is it just *my* shit he doesn't like?'

'I realise that you might not be the only, um, contributor to the problem,' intoned the mayor. 'But apparently M. Rey has provided the Bureau with pictures of your drains discharging into the stream.' He waved his hands in the air again, this time as if to say, 'So you're scuppered.' I could not avoid the impression that he was letting it be known that he considered all of this absurd, and none of his fault.

Slowly – you know I am a bit thick sometimes – I came to realise that this had nothing to do with the European Directive at all. This was a dispute – and apparently a bitter one with no love lost on either side – between two neighbours on the point of who had the right to shit where. And the good mayor was sick to the back teeth of it and the position it had put him in.

I was still taking this in, when a voice from behind me said. 'Will Bardeau be made to put in a septic tank?' A rumble from the gathering indicated that this was what most of them were concerned about.

'I don't know,' replied the mayor. 'His property is outside the urbanised zone of the village, so I think he might be.'

'*Zut!* If he's made to put in a septic tank, then we'll all have to,' exclaimed another. 'Where the hell am I supposed to put one? This will cost us a fortune.'

Another put in, 'It's outrageous. All because that clown Rey doesn't like a little bit of shit on his cattle.'

'Ah, monsieur, you know, these are dairy cattle, and the regulations these days...' The mayor wagged his finger. 'It's Europe, you know.'

'Bah, so he has to wash his damn cows before he milks them. So what? We all do. They manage to get themselves well enough covered in their own shit.'

'I told you! Bloody ponce doesn't like *my* shit, that's all,' cried M. Bardeau, leaping to his feet again.

'Well, there's more fat in it than cowshit, that's for sure!' (M Bardeau was not, by any stretch of the imagination, a slender figure.)

'Yes, and more alcohol in his piss too,' came another response.

I could see that the poor M. Bardeau was struggling for a witty response but the drink was getting in his way. '*Bah, quelle merde,*' he exclaimed, before his companions dragged him back down to his seat. I think they were afraid he might measure his length.

The mayor shook his head, like a father surveying the scene after his children have finished a food-fight. 'Do I take it, then, that we are going to do nothing? Do you want to hand responsibility for the matter over to the Bureau?' He gazed seriously at the assembly. 'Because something is going to have to be done. It has gone to the *Departement*.'

There came a grumbling that I took to mean dissent in the ranks, and the mayor sighed. 'Look, either we come up with a concrete proposal or we let the Bureau decide what to do.' He shrugged. 'My hands are tied.'

'Who pays if we leave it to them?' came a voice.

'It depends on whose responsibility it is. If the Bureau decides it's our responsibility, we'll have to pay for the work. If they decide Bardeau's at fault, he'll have to fix it. If they decide it's their problem, they pay.' The mayor shrugged again, this time as if to say, 'It's in the lap of the gods.'

'And if we decide to do it ourselves?'

'The same.'

'So whether or not we decide to do something won't affect who pays for it?'

'No. The work would have to be done to the Bureau's standards anyway.'

'Well, the decision's taken, as far as I'm concerned. Let them do the bloody work, I have enough to worry about.'

'What about me?' wailed Bardeau. 'Don't I get a say? What if they say I have to put in a septic tank?'

'Ah, you can stuff it – you'll wheedle a grant for a septic tank, I'll bet. Serves you right for causing all this trouble in the first place. You would piss down the river on Rey just for the pleasure of pissing on the stuck-up git, you would.' A general noise of approval indicated that, whether or not the rest of the company would actually have gone to the lengths of pissing on M. Rey, the general estimation of his character was agreed with by all them.

'Stuck up? You can say that again. Why isn't he here tonight?'

'Maybe because he knows he might "fall down" on the way home. And that would serve him right for getting the bloody *Departement* snooping around. Like we didn't have enough of them already.'

'Yes, they're like the *flics*, that lot – they always find something.'

The mood had obviously lightened, and even M Bardeau had cheered up. He seemed happier with my presence, though I was completely at a loss as to why he had been so hostile in the first place, or now, was being positively affable. Indeed he deliberately caught my eye and smiled.

After I thought about it I realised what had happened; the poor man was expecting to be hauled over the coals for provoking his neighbour into calling in the dreaded Bureau. The thought was so shameful he'd even got drunk beforehand; to be given a drubbing with an *Anglais* present was just too much for him to bear.

However, I had a hunch that my presence had in fact protected him. The other men at the meeting (and they were all men,) had been constrained in their attacks simply by the fact that I was there. Being a foreigner – and dressed in a suit at that – they had decided they'd better behave in front of me. Instead, the hapless – and absent – M. Rey was the target for their ire. I'd no doubt Bardeau would get his ears bent later, but for the moment, although he wasn't getting any sympathy, (I doubt he expected much,) at least he wasn't being publicly vilified.

'That's it, then,' intoned the mayor. 'We are officially deciding to do nothing, again, and so hand responsibility over to the Bureau?'

There was a noise that signified assent. The mayor banged the table with his gavel, and said 'Good.' There was a tone in his voice that suggested to me that he really meant it too, and I suppose after twenty years of listening to two men bickering about shit, he was justified.

The meeting began to break up, with most of the men bending their paths towards the cafe. It looked to be a busy night. In some considerable confusion, but greatly amused, I made my way home to tell Moira all about the meeting.

Later that month, little, official-looking vans began to appear in the village and worryingly official-looking men began taking notes and comparing measurements with the *cadastre*. Then all was quiet for several months and the whole village held its breath, not least I. What would happen? Would we all have to put in septic tanks? Where would we put in a septic tank? How much would it all cost? And who was going to have to pay for it?

At least there was a silver lining of some sorts – surely, now, the river would be cleaned up.

Then, one day, I turned right at the shop, intending to head for Nolay, and found that the road was blocked, with a diversion via Santosse. I could see a digger ripping up the culvert at the bottom of M. Rey's field. Later, when I got back from town, I went to examine what they'd been up to.

They had removed the old two-foot diameter tube that led the little stream under the road, and replaced it with a four-foot diameter one; and then they had neatly re-laid the carriageway. It was an impressively good job too.

As usual, I sought advice from Antoine le Potier. To this day, Antoine regards me as being on a point on a scale somewhere between 'eccentric' and 'certifiable,' but since he deliberately ploughs a highly idiosyncratic furrow himself, this has boosted our friendship rather than discouraged it. He has ever been my weather-vane on the mysteries of the darkest Arrière-côte.

'That's it?' I asked, over *aperos*.

He nodded. 'Yes. Now the field won't flood in winter and Rey's cattle won't be up to their knees in Bardeau's shit.'

'But the shit will still be in the river,' I observed.

'Yes, but that was not the complaint. The complaint was that the cows got covered in shit – now they won't. Job done.'

I pondered this disconsolately. It looked as though poor Calum was not going to be paddling in the river that summer. Again. 'And who pays?'

'Oh, the *Departement* will pay. It wasn't a sanitation matter at all, you see. Drainage is the village's responsibility, but the problem was caused because the culvert under the road was too small. The roads are the *Departement's* responsibility, so it was the *Departement's* problem, and they had to fix it.'

'What about the European Directive?'

Antoine just shrugged.

By the way, M. Bardeau became a good friend. He and his wife and daughter were really charming people, and very kind to us. I did eventually meet the reclusive M. Rey, and found him polite and friendly and not at all stuck-up; indeed very innocuous. But I discovered later that his father and mother had been incomers to the village, from Bligny.

And everyone in P'tit Moulin knows that people from Bligny are *all* stuck-up.

Now, while we are on the subject of Clan Bardeau, I am reminded of another little yarn. His was one of two farms in the village which, in the 90s, sold milk at the gate. You took along your little aluminium pitcher and they would fill it. Nice it was too.

I liked to buy milk this way because I had worked in dairy years before and I have a taste for what the French call *'lait cru'*. That is, unpasteurised milk. In those days the only milk you could get at supermarkets was the sterilised UHT stuff, which is okay, you know, but it doesn't really taste very much like milk.

Of course, we boiled the local milk before giving it to our children, but I was inclined to take a mug from the pitcher for myself, nice and raw.

After a couple of severe bouts of some gastric illness that, I insisted, had nothing at all to do with the milk, I came to accept Moira's logic – 'So why are you the only one who's sick?'

I stopped buying my milk at the closer farm and instead went to the Bardeau's. I think I finally realised that the ghastly, filthy rag the first lot were using to clean off udders was not really going to do the job. I mean I am a qualified Dairy Herdsman, I know about these things.

Bardeau's was at least more approximate to the standards considered normal in the late 20th century. It wasn't the sparkling palace of hygiene that I had worked in, but it was close. Well, closer, at least.

Monsieur Bardeau, though he would always greet me, never dealt with the milk. It was always his wife, Madame Bardeau, or his daughter, Mademoiselle Bardeau, who did that. (This French stuff is easy when you know how.) By the way, M. Bardeau is now past-tense but his good lady wife is still around, and still as friendly. The farm is run by mademoiselle, who remains resolutely, Mademoiselle Bardeau.

I always hoped it would be the daughter who would serve me. This was not because of my admitted excess of urge...well, not only that. She is a fine looking woman, in my defence.

There was a more pressing reason. Madame Bardeau – who, by the way, always had her hair dyed but insisted on leaving it until her pure-white roots were an inch long before repeating – appeared to have some insidious form of rhinitis.

In other words. she had a perpetual sniffle. It didn't seem to matter what season of the year it was, Madame Bardeau constantly had a drip hanging from the end of her nose.

Now, the procedure for buying milk *chez* Bardeau was that one would go into the farmhouse kitchen where the milk for sale 'over the gate' was kept cool, in the fridge. Madame Bardeau would take out the churn, place it on the kitchen table, take off the lid, stir it with a plastic spatula and then use a stainless steel ladle to transfer it into a measuring jar, and thence into the customer's pitcher. Sounds OK, yes? And even my uppity notions of dairy-herd-management-Bicton-College-style cleanliness were not offended.

The kitchen was clean...well, it didn't smell, anyway. The fridge did not have obvious mould; the churn looked okay and the various stirring and ladling instruments also. Even the measuring jar was obviously freshly washed.

Yet I was always in direst trepidation when I bought the milk.

The reason was that drip on the end of Madame Bardeau's nose. There seemed a limitless number of possible moments when it could fall off and end up in the milk; an infinite variety of manners in which I could end up with a pitcher of milk containing a part – and not a very pleasant one – of the good lady.

She, by the way, seemed oblivious to her drip, almost as if it were not there. I, on the other hand, was fascinated, nay, mesmerised by it.

Croutons and Cheese!

Every time her head moved, the drip would wobble and my terror would increase. And though I never actually saw a drip fall, I was haunted by them, lay awake at night worrying about them.

I have to admit that I am a coward: when I bought from Madame, rather than Madamoiselle, even though I had watched her drip with hawk-eyes, willing it to stay put on the end of her nose, I never drank the milk unboiled. Just a step too far, that was.

Now the clever Bardeau women did not just have milk for sale, they also made *faisselle,* which is a kind of cheese, and even butter, both of which were very good. So, turning my back on the question of drips and the unlimited possibilities for getting said drips in the produce, I used to buy both. I mean, you can buy them at the supermarket, but I like to support local enterprises.

The butter was really nice and though I don't often eat it, Moira liked it for cooking. She said it had a better flavour than the shop stuff, and I agreed.

Now *faisselle* is a milk cheese that you eat fresh. It's very mild in flavour and soft. It's wet; in English I think it might be called 'curd cheese'. The point is that the whey (the liquid part) is still in it.

Most people eat their *faisselle* just like that but I prefer a bit of consistency in my cheese, so I used to keep mine a little longer, a week to ten days. It kinda grew a skin and stiffened up a bit. The texture was better (I think) and the flavour was definitely stronger.

I even bought a little cheese-safe to hang in the cellar so the cheeses would be safe from flies and other pests. Only a true vulgarian keeps cheese in the fridge.

One day I was preparing the wine for lunch when I heard a yelp coming from the direction of the cellar. Readers will appreciate by now that I tended to take Moira's yelps seriously, so they'll know that I lost no time in responding.

When I got there she was squinting intensely into the cheese-safe. 'What is it?

'That cheese is alive,' she said.

Well, technically, cheese is alive, you know. It's a bacteria paradise. But that was not what Moira meant at all. 'Look at the skin. It's moving.'

I looked – it's a little dim the cellar, but sure enough, the skin was definitely moving.

French Onion Soup! II

Beginning to develop an incipient case of the total heebee-jeebies, I opened the safe and removed the cheese, on the plate it sat on. These I ferried to the courtyard. Best to do these things outside.

Close inspection showed that the skin of the *faisselle* was covered in squirming white worms. They were about four millimetres long.

I thought about it a while. There was no other cheese in the house and it was past 12, so the nearest supermarket would be closed. Shrugging my shoulders, I took a knife, scraped off the skin – with the worms – and gave it to the dogs. The rest – much to Moira's undisguised horror – I ate.

I never bought Madame Bardeau's *faisselle* again.

The Stove Story

Life certainly is an interesting tapestry here in P'tit Moulin. One morning I was awakened at some ungodly hour – well, just before nine actually, but I am semi-nocturnal – by an excessively enthusiastic clangour (good word that) of my front door bell, of which more later.

Well, I threw on a pair of jeans and a T and went to see who had disturbed the peace in this manner, and there on my doorstep was a rather scruffy individual, definitely of the traditional French horny-handed persuasion. Behind him was a truck that looked, to my bleary and unaided vision, even older and more dilapidated than my Isuzu, and that's saying something.

He must have recognised my absence of recognition. 'Monsieur,' he said, 'The last time I passed you said you had some scrap.' (In French of course, I'm just trying to make it easy for you. Do keep up.)

A moment for that to clatter down through the various depths of the Fleming brain and I realised that the august personage on my doorstep was none other than that rough diamond, the local scrap-metal man, a Stephan. (You'll find out.)

Actually his yard is in Seurre, on the other side of Beaune and he travels around in his beaten-up truck, tinkling a little bell to alert those desiring to be rid of things, interesting to scrap-metal men, of his presence among them.

We are quite well off for rough diamonds of that ilk here, so I may perhaps be forgiven for not identifying this one more quickly. Plus I am as blind as a bat without my lenses in. Although bats apparently see quite well. Funny that.

Anyway, I remembered. I changed over the *ballon chauffe-eau,* better known as the immersion (hot water tank for you…tanks…) when the last one gave up under the relentless assault of water so hard you'd think landing ducks would bounce. The old one had been cluttering up my garage, and so serving as the perfect pretext for me not to bother cleaning the damn place up, since November last.

Stopping only to grab a pair of galoshes, I headed for the barn, and minutes later, the horrible object, along with a few other items, was in the back of his truck. We shook hands and I considered what to do next.

I was just in the process of oiling the cogitation with coffee, when the bell rang again, more timidly this time. It turned out to be my neighbour but one.

'Can you help?' quoth she, 'The scrap man needs a hand to load my old stove.'

Well, we all help each other out here, it is rural France, and so off I went with her. Now you see, I had an old Godin stove in the bedroom upstairs, but it was completely kaput and filled the room with smoke, so I had thrown that in the garage around the same time as the *ballon chauffe-eau* got chucked in there. The only difference was that I had earmarked the Godin for eventual repair and refurbishment. (Yeah, like that was ever going to happen, I know. You don't have to be so blunt about it.)

Where was I? Oh yes. Anyway, my neighbour's, while needing a good clean and lick of stove-black (anyone else remember Zebrite? That stuff) was in pretty much perfect condition, so without second thought, I said, 'Gosh, I'd like that!'

My neighbour shrugged and nodded. 'Sure,' she said. 'You'll need to shift it though.'

As I glanced round I could see that there was a problem, from the crestfallen look on our loyal scrappy's phizog. 'Wait a minute,' I said. 'I have another one just like that – you can have that one instead.'

The price of scrap must be high just now, because you'd have thought I'd given the bugger money. Lickety-split he reversed his truck, in a cloud of blue smoke, back up to my place. (It was actually much worse than my Isuzu, I could see now I had my lenses in.)

Anyway, after lunch I hied me down to my neighbour's with my trusty two-wheeled sack truck, and, not without effort and swearing, got it back *chez moi*. Where I was confronted with another problem. The damn thing must weigh 300 pounds – how was I going to get it up the stairs? A couple of tentative efforts made it clear that it was not going to be easy – and I am not small, like.

So I decided to have another cogitate with some coffee. Should I dismantle it? Looking at the rusted bolts did not inspire confidence, but I wasn't going to have it fall down a spiral stone staircase on top of me. Really, it needed two men; the job would be easy that way, one lifting at the bottom and the other pulling and steadying. I thought of asking Antoine, my friend the potter, but he was away and anyway I like to have a few favours banked with him. Then suddenly, it clicked: an old friend had, just a few nights before, called to take me up on the open invite to come and visit. Perfect. He could help me up the stairs with my stove…P'tit Moulin is like that, you know. Everything just falls into place.

Except now I suppose I'll have to tidy up the barn. Oh well.

I did promise more about the bell. For years we had no doorbell, and everybody complained we never answered the door, which was probably true. However the thought of drilling through metre-thick walls to wire in a doorbell…nah. So last year I went modern and bought a wireless one. It worked by radio, see? Anyway I duly installed it and basked in my efficiency and handiness. Then one day my neighbour (another one) texted me the bad news. 'Your doorbell doesn't work. I've been ringing it for 20 minutes.'

She was right, too. I checked the batteries – all fine. Not that. Fiendish thing had packed up. Serves me right for buying it in Lidl, I suppose. Anyway, enough of that nonsense. I had sold my sailing-yacht the year before and one of the few things I kept was the bell, which was a typical piece of chandlery tat. Now I saw a use, and it was duly screwed to the front door.

And that is how the scrap man was able to make enough row to wake me from my slumbers that morning.

Black Economy

This seems about as appropriate a moment as any to discuss the Black Economy. You see, your loyal Frenchman hates *l'Administration* with a passion, and will at every opportunity attempt to get one over. Since *l'Administration* has no liking for having one got over on it, the result is a confrontation, with most French citizens doing everything they can to avoid paying taxes, which they regard as little better than robbery, and *l'Administration* taking the view that all French citizens are basically crooks, and adopting tactics to match.

Now it is of course, a matter of perspective. To give an example, it has always been the custom of the good folks of St Andrews in Scotland to let out spare rooms during that great golfing festival, the Open. (In fact, it is not at all unknown for them to decamp to caravans in the back garden and let out the whole house.) For most of the good burghers of that ancient town, this amounted to a nice little windfall, which they slipped into their hippers without a second thought. Imagine the consternation when representatives of Her Majesty's Inland Revenue, as it was then, were spotted in the streets of that fair town, taking note of the houses that had 'Rooms for Let' notices. It even made the front page of the *Daily Record*.

Well in France it's about a million times more so, and the enforcement are not nice young girls with slightly old-fashioned dress-sense and perhaps just a few too many pounds on the hips, but the police. Armed police, at that.

The fact that *les flics* are the ones charged with seeking out and recovering unpaid tax, of course, just makes your Frenchman, ever loyal to the anarchistic foundations of Revolution upon which he believes the Glorious Republic to be built, even more determined to avoid paying tax on something – anything – as a matter of principle. The fact that these particular *flics* are also qualified accountants – and so ineffably bourgeois – just makes the whole thing worse.

The situation is compounded by the infernal system of Social Security charges. These amount to a huge deterrent to registering a business with the tax authorities, and if you happen to have the kind of business that can happily work in cash, well then. And *l'Administration* has proved singularly inept at finding ways to sweeten the bitter pill of registration. The result is that all over France, countless joiners, build-

Croutons and Cheese!

ers, gardeners, handymen and others, all so necessary to the smooth running of life, will only take payment in cash, much to the fury of the legitimate businesses who are paying the charges and who therefore have to ask twice as much for their services.

Yet, if you ever ask about anything like this, the French will, to a man, say 'But you must obey the law,' while blatantly and deliberately ignoring it themselves, at every possible opportunity.

You think I exaggerate? You think that old fool has been drinking too much cheap red plonk?

Consider this: in the mid 1990s a bemused French public was confronted by a series of advertisements promoting a new kind of cheque. This was a very clever thing, they said, which would allow you to pay for casual work quite legally. How so? Well, you got your black-economy handyman to come out and clear your gutters or tidy up the policies and when he was done, you used a special cheque-book – free from your bank – to pay him. And then, when he cashed the cheque, he got his money, minus an element for the taxes and charges he was supposed to pay. When the cheque came back to your bank, they debited the money plus an element to cover the taxes and charges that the employer – that is to say you – was supposed to pay. All worked out automatically and you didn't even have to lift a calculator. My goodness, what a whizz of an idea. Of course! The charges would be paid, so no-one was breaking the law.

You know, it is said that an Anglo-Saxon engineer, when confronted by a new idea, will say, 'Well, the theory might be fine, but does it work in practise?' His (or her) French engineer cousin will look at a new machine and sniffily say, 'Well, of course I can see that it *works,* but does the theory hold up?' It's an amusing little anecdote that has more than a dash of truth in it.

And the story of the cheques suffers from the same problem. The idea works perfectly in theory – everyone is paid and no-one breaks the law. It is in the practicalities that it fails, for in the first place, no-one in the black economy is going to be daft enough to accept a cheque, far less bank it – oh no, sirree, that is a cash-only system. And in any case, any home-owner prepared to pay the full whack – which is what the system arranges, willy-nilly – will just call up one of the legitimate enterprises in the phone book, rather than employ someone 'on the black.'

See, what Governments never really understand, although they might say they do, is that people really like to get away with a bit of tax evasion. It makes life that much sweeter – not only do you get the job done, you get it done cheap because it's done black. This is such a satisfying experience that we even get work done that we had no intention of getting done, and wouldn't, except that it is such a good deal – *because it's black*.

For most of us, this probably amounts to an insignificant sum every year. Suppose Paddy and his mates heave round the end of your drive, say they've noticed said drive is a bit worn-out looking and offer you a coat of new tarmac for £250 cash, no questions asked. Well the very last thing you'll do is worry about who's going to pay the damn tax. Instead you rub your hands in glee and nip down to the hole in the wall to get the readies and think it a cracking deal at that. So what if the car park at the new supermarket ends up a couple of thou under specified depth? You don't shop at Tesco's anyway. (Or wherever.) And who the hell cares if the Exchequer is out a few imaginary quid? The bhoys are being taxed plenty on their earnings, and so are you. If they dumped the tarmac because you didn't want it, or it ended up spread all over the Tesco car park, the taxman would not see the first penny more. So what's the harm?

Unfortunately, however, the Exchequer seems to disagree, probably because its bean-counters add up all the imaginary few quid that they wouldn't get anyway. Then they find it comes to a few billion imaginary quid a year. Oh dear, they gasp, can't have that, ignoring the fact that the money they are talking about is completely non-existent. It could never, ever find its way into their groaning coffers, since if they forced us all to pay tax on it, the tax-generating transaction itself would *simply never take place*.

Paddy and the bhoys would just put an another millimetre on the car-park with the extra black stuff – if they don't dump it behind your hedge on the QT – and then go for a few pints. And instead of being in the good books with the missus for once, you'll wait another ten years, till the thistles are growing through it, to do anything at all about that drive of yours – no matter how much she moans. Silly buggers; imaginary money is just imaginary money! Try paying the mortgage with it and see how far you get. We would all be billionaires with the taxman's kind of logic. Still, some politicians like that sort of bull – which on second thought, tells me all I want to know.

So *'le noir'* is a big business in France. I don't know how big – surprisingly enough, no official stats are kept. In Italy, it has been estimated that as much as 55% of the economy is black. It's funny, though; I can remember discussing this back in Blighty with a client, who came over all shocked by such foreign delinquency. I gave him my bill and he immediately said, 'Any discount for cash?' I don't think the irony was quite apparent to him. (And naturally, I declined his offer to be complicit in such nefariousness.)

Round here, you have a choice: you can have a legit tradesman for 50 Euros an hour or one *au noir* for 25. Your choice. It could actually be the same guy.

To be fair, *l'Administration* has made efforts to make things easier for small businesses. It has reduced the burden of accountability and at last ensured that one is not bankrupted by charges set at a level one's business cannot hope to meet. But it's not easy the way it is in UK.

For example, one of the ladies in the village here at P'tit Moulin wanted to set up a little stall at the end of her path. She proposed to sell honey, produce from her garden and various knick-knacks that she bought in flea-markets, from it. Oh, no, she couldn't. She would have to have a *commercants'* licence, be registered, pay *les charges*…She was semi-retired and she might possibly have made 20 Euros a week pocket-money. But that was stifled right away. France is not a land of entrepreneurial delight, even though they nod their heads as enthusiastically as those dogs you used to see in car rear windows and say that, 'Oh, yes it is.' It has many charms, delights and much to commend it generally, but it doesn't favour the free market. Not at all.

However, let us leave that aside and return to the arrival of the new millennium and that great milestone of European integration, the Euro. You would not have thought that the simple change of a currency would trigger an economic boom, would you? But it did. Would you like to know why?

Well, one of the methods used by *l'Administration* to keep tabs on the loyal citizenry was that all transactions over 5000 francs were supposed to be paid by cheque, because a cheque is traceable. Nowadays, since that seems not to have worked too well, they have reduced the amount to 300 Euros. That's less than half the previous amount.

The problem is that the French Tax Police have the absolute right to immediate access to anyone's banking records. That's without requirement for a warrant, court order, by-your-leave or even reasonable ground for suspicion. So they can spot any income that doesn't appear on the account-holder's tax return.

The French are not thick, so they adopted a simple policy: ignore the law. All sorts of payments continued to be made in cash, contributing to the thriving black economy. But what to do with it? One could hardly put it in the bank, after all, since any cash payment of more than five thousand francs was automatically flagged for investigation.

So for years the loyal French salted it away under floorboards, inside mattresses, behind loose bricks in walls, in pots in their kitchens, in the loft, under the wine in their *caves*, in holes in trees and buried under the ground (I am not kidding). Anywhere, in fact, where there was a decent chance the Tax Police would not find it. And all went swimmingly.

The quiet accumulation of undeclared wealth, the right of every enterprising citizen, continued apace and no-one ever saw a reason why it should end. Enough tax was being paid to keep the country running, the people had their little stashes of black money, always the most satisfying kind, and while the Tax Police knew damn fine they were being hoodwinked, nobody else cared.

And then, and then. The Euro. Everyone was so keen on it too; it was a milestone, a landmark, a great step forward in the European Project. And then they realised – what were they going to do with all that cash under the bed? They could hardly change it at the bank. Heaven forfend, there would be no end of ructions and questions about where it had come from. Inevitably there would be tax to pay and most likely fines and penalties to boot. And after E-day, as this catastrophe was to be known, the only place you could change your francs for Euros would *be* at the bank.

It was a classic rock-and-a-hard-place dilemma.

Only one thing for it. Spend the lot. There is no Frenchman alive who would not rather blow the black money he had spent years, perhaps decades, accumulating on wine, cigarettes, a new car, or a present for his mistress, than give it to the cursed *Administration*.

And so, dear reader, it was. In the closing months of 2001 the air was filled with a febrile anxiety. Shopkeepers reported the best Christmas buying spree they could ever remember; but it did not end there. No, that was only the beginning. The Euro officially supplanted the franc on the first of January 2002, but the loyal citizenry were given unto the end

Croutons and Cheese!

of February to spend, spend, spend their old francs. Which they did.

Having realised that there was no way they could hold on to their hard-earned black money, and that it was impossible to put it in the bank, they spent with an enthusiasm only a Frenchman on a mission knows. New cars were everywhere and even in P'tit Moulin, shiny new white Renault vans were purchased to replace the worn-out old bangers that had somehow been kept going for years. Roofs that had leaked buckets for decades were clad in beautiful new tiles, and many were the French ladies who stepped out in new fur coats.

Whether these were presents from their guilty husbands or doting lovers is neither here nor there.

Animal Anecdotes

During our first sojourn in the wine and sun-soaked idyll of P'tit Moulin (we shall ignore the cowshit liberally applied to the roads), our first son, Calum, became the owner of a cat. Well, it wasn't really *his* cat, you know, but he liked to pretend it was. Pete and Sharon's cat had kittens and we were blackmailed into giving one a home. It's very hard to resist when someone shoves a tiny orange bundle into your hands and says 'Take it, it's yours.' They always make sure the kids are present, I have noticed.

Anyway, we accepted and a very cute wee thing he was too, a tiny ginger tom whom Calum promptly named 'Speed Christmas Sherry'. He always did have a way with names, that lad. The little chap arrived on Christmas day, which explains part of the name. Six weeks old and full of mischief. Our two dogs adopted him immediately and so did we.

It soon transpired that the feline addition to the latest family of Moulinards was something of an adventurer, and had unforeseen talents.

At that time our principal heating in the *grande salle* on the ground floor was by a huge De Ville woodburning cooker, which loyal readers may remember from the first book in this series. Not only was this capable of getting the room to the kind of fug that made rapid movement undesirable (or maybe that was the wine) it was also a very effective hotplate; even if the oven did tend to make everything wood-ash flavoured.

Speed Christmas Sherry was a bright and curious kitten and obviously wondered what on earth was going on up there on top of the stove, where all the magical smells were coming from. So one day he decided to have a look.

Now cats do this all the time, usually when their humans are not looking, but most modern cookers do not have a top plate permanently at a temperature where spit will bounce – 250 degrees Celsius, I am reliably informed.

It was like one of those slow-motion videos, which no-one could do anything to prevent. We stared, aghast, as the curious orange adventurer jumped on to the hot plate, catapulted vertically into the air, hung there for a moment, came back down again, discovered the hotplate had not cooled, ricocheted sideways (realising that spending all day pretending to be a yo-yo was dull) with a blood-curdling yowl and disappeared under the table.

Immediate panic ensued. Calum, after some time, managed to get Sherry (for short) out from under the table. My first-aid instincts were to arrange for him to stand in a basin of cold water filled with ice-cubes, but Moira just gave me one of the looks they used to call 'old-fashioned'. I suppose, in hindsight, it might be quite tricky to get a kitten to do that. But you know how pragmatic I am.

So into his basket he went and we all trooped off to the vet, who, fortunately, was in. He gave me the Look when I explained what had happened, which I had rather been expecting. His manner let me know I had been a very irresponsible cat owner indeed. I thought this a little unfair. After all, I hadn't put the little sod there. It was all his idea.

Anyway it turned out that, miraculously, he had suffered only superficial burns, and the good vet returned him to the care of his mad owners with several admonishments about keeping him away from the stove.

Like he was ever going to try that again. Cats might have tiny little brains but that doesn't mean they're stupid.

This was not the last time I was obliged to open my wallet because of the antics of Mr Sherry, who, I hasten to add, in order to soothe the nerves of cat-loving readers, made a full recovery from his toe-toasting very quickly. He returned to being an inveterate little pest – or delight, depending.

The De Ville consumed a great deal of wood and just keeping it going took a full morning's work every week, carting logs down from the field, sawing them to length, chopping them up and stacking the logs. Well, one could have done it in two hours, I suppose, but there are all those refreshment breaks. One does not move to the halcyon idyll of rural France to work like a troglodyte, after all.

This was our second winter in P'tit Moulin and I had bought a large quantity of oak squarings from the local sawmill, an excellent method of heating. They say, in P'tit Moulin, that wood has the unique ability to heat you up six times: once when you fell it, once when you stack it, once when you bring it down from the woods, once when you saw it, once when you chop it and once when you burn it. Very efficient, wood is.

And on a more serious note, since it is technically morning and I am still on coffee, wood is a most excellent source of heat from an environmental perspective. Although there is the small question of particulate emissions – smoke, do keep up – in principle, wood is very green and tree-huggy. The trees grow and absorb carbon, then you cut them down and release it. Then the same thing happens again.

This, as the more alert of you will have spotted, does not take into account the fuel used to cut and transport the wood from forest to home. Nor does it, for that matter, account for the *pneus* that were traditionally used up the woods to light the fires and burn off the hag. I am pleased to report that these days, the horny-handed woodloppers just leave this to rot away, which puts the nutrients back in the soil. Much more eco, but not so good for the roast chickens I described in the last volume.

What that means, I would take a moment to point out, is that the less moving around of timber that one does, the better. The modern fashion of carting it away to some distant factory to be turned into pellets and then carting it back, to sell to those thick enough to pay the prices demanded, is both ecologically unsound and ludicrously expensive. But that is how Capitalism works: screw the environment, let's make money.

Anyway, we stacked the chopped timber, which I spent every Sunday morning preparing, in a lean-to in the courtyard. Once every couple of days I would stack up the piles beside the various stoves we were using, mainly of course the De Ville. In winter this meant bringing a fair bit of mud in from the courtyard ('trailing gutters in', my grandmother would have said.) In order not to make the floors too filthy we had flattened a number of huge cardboard boxes that we laid on the tiles to form a walkway. Once the stacking of the firewood was done, they were folded up till next time and the tiles did not suffer a bit.

Once, while I was doing this, a big basket of logs in my brawny arms, I was sure – nay could swear – I heard a muffled crunch followed by a squeak from under the cardboard. Being male, I thought little of this.

Only later did Calum pipe up that he could not find Sherry. This was hardly unusual, so I didn't think much of that either, and instead focussed on finishing the logs and having a beer. (It is a strange irony that one expends so much effort getting warm, but still enjoys a cold beer, *n'est-ce pas?*)

However, when said cat was found, he didn't look quite right. Sort of out of shape, you might say. Distinctly winded.

'Daddy,' howled Calum, 'You *stood* on him!'

Well the little pest shouldn't have been fossicking around under the cardboard, I thought, but had the presence of mind (aware the Moira was watching me) to phrase my response differently.

'Is he all right?' I solicited.

'I don't know,' replied Moira, with an air that confirmed this was my fault. Like I had x-ray vision.

Talking of x-rays, that is what I ended up forking out for, together with an overnight 'for observation' at the vet. Who did not hesitate to let me know I was still unfit to own a cat.

It turned out that Sherry may have used two of his lives, but he had withstood being trodden on by a 15-stone Scot carrying another two stones of logs with apparently no lasting damage. I wish my wallet had been as lucky.

The Firemen and the Flying Cat

Talking of cats reminds me of another incident, this time up the road at Ivry en Montagne, where, as you may recall, my friend Antoine *le Potier* resides.

Now Antoine is a pacifist and as such, when he had received the call-up to National Service, he had refused to join the army. The French, being practical, did not get all uppity about Conscientious Objectors, but instead offered programmes of voluntary work for them. The downside was that service in the army only lasted one year while the voluntary work lasted two. Nevertheless, Antoine had opted for the latter, and had spent his time aiding the homeless.

His completion of National Service made him eligible to be part of the volunteer fire brigade, and being a concerned citizen, as well as a big kid who loved fire engines, he adopted this role enthusiastically.

In all the villages in those days there were volunteer fire brigades. This gave rise to a delightful French expression: *peté comme un pompier* – 'pissed as a fireman' and having once or twice followed fire engines on their way to an emergency, I can attest to the accuracy of this aphorism. The idea was that the boys had been in the cafe when the alarm went off, and you know what we do in the cafes, don't you?

Perhaps because of this, the volunteer fire brigades, with their little ex-military fire engines, have now all been disbanded. They have been replaced with proper professional fire brigades who have huge shiny red fire-engines, a wonder to behold. Or perhaps, more pragmatically, it is just that fire personnel these days have to be much better trained. And no drinking in the cafe before call-out.

One day, before this leap into modernity occurred, we were *chez* Antoine when an English woman appeared at the door. She was renting a *gite* in the village and was very concerned that there was a cat stuck at the top of a pine tree in the garden.

She had been directed to Antoine, since he was responsible for all waifs, strays and *Anglais* who needed assistance in Ivry, apparently. The lady, whose name I forget, was very concerned. She was delighted that we were present, since this meant she did not have to try to speak French. It was something she did not do too well.

'It's been up there for three days, you know,' she explained, all animal concern. 'It might starve, or die of thirst or something.'

Croutons and Cheese!

Now I could tell that Antoine was less than impressed by this, but he realised that if he did not do something about the arboreal feline, he would never be rid of the crazy cat lady. So, with an air of great patience and sympathy (one must humour *les Anglais*; it's not their fault and they are our guests), he rose to the challenge.

'It's all right,' he said. 'I will come and 'ave a look.'

Naturally, this meant that he, his wife and kids, we and our kids and several others who happened to be around, all went to look too; this is France, after all.

The cat was, indeed, at the very top of a very tall pine tree. It was 25 metres or more up, and wailing pitifully. Antoine nodded and sucked his tooth as the English lady explained again that it had been up there for three days and so on. Then he turned to me, and said, in French, 'The damn cat will come down when it gets hungry enough. But we had better do something anyway.'

'I will call the fire brigade,' he said to the lady, and withdrew.

I could tell she was impressed. It was a very tall tree. 'They have a ladder long enough to get all the way up there? Gosh.'

I was aware that a crowd was gathering and realised they had all come along to see The Show. The jungle telegraph is very effective in these parts. An air of carnival pervaded the atmosphere.

At length we heard the siren and knew that help was at hand. Moments later, the fire engine appeared, driven by Antoine, and drew up alongside. The crew – all local men of course – hopped out and began discussing the issue in serious voices. Eventually the lads – all in uniform and wearing the most glorious fire-fighters' helmets I have ever seen – arrived at a consensus, and Things Began to Happen.

'What are they going to do?' hissed the English lady, who had now been joined by her husband. 'That ladder isn't nearly long enough...'

Meanwhile some of the lads were busy rolling out three-inch fire hose on the road (Well okay, 75mm if you must.) They hooked up the pump on the fire engine to the nearest fire hydrant and were soon rolling out more hose toward the tree. I could see the English lady's eyes begin to narrow and her expression changed to one of consternation.

The boys were now ready and a team of three took the hose while Antoine signalled the pump operator. The machine roared and the earth shook; and then the hose team opened the valve and sent a jet of high-pressure water arcing into the sky.

The tree bent radically under the assault of the deluge and within two twitches of a cat's tail (sorry) our arboreal – and now drenched – cat became an aviating feline as it was squirted out of the branches, flew through the air and came down on the grass at the bottom. It's true about cats always landing on their feet, you know. It shot its rescuers a look of pure, waterlogged evil and disappeared into the shrubbery.

A round of applause broke out from the crowd and there was much clapping of backs and shaking of hands. The fire brigade began rolling up the hoses and looking efficient, while Antoine took it all in his stride. I had the distinct impression that this was not the first time he had done this.

Describing the look on the English lady's face is difficult. Mortified, perhaps. Disillusioned, maybe. But whatever it was, we had little time to worry, and left comforting her to her husband, who was similarly aghast, as Antoine came up.

'We're going to put the fire engine away then have a glass of wine. Care to join us?'

And why ever not?

The Throat Holder-Upper

When we first arrived in France, Moira, as you may recall, was pregnant to the back teeth, as the French saying goes. We've already mentioned the fun we had with the excellent French health system, but this is a more light-hearted pregnancy-related story.

As the big day loomed nearer, Moira realised that she needed nursing bras. (Whether she did or not is another topic altogether; it turns out that bras are a cultural rather than a physical requirement.) However in those days we were much more politically naïve than now, so off we went, Moira and me and Calum, to Chalon sur Saone to locate and purchase this wonder of technology.

There was a problem. Back then, I confess, my French was restricted and that may have been partly responsible.

The centre of Chalon is beautiful and medieval, surrounded by later quarters. It's a bit like a slice through an onion. We headed for the old part to look for a shop. We knew what we were looking for and we thought we knew where to locate it: a maternity shop. We couldn't find one of those at first so I decided to ask. At the time, Moira's French was, erm, basic.

So we sauntered into what looked like the French equivalent of Top Shop. A smiling if somewhat wary assistant hove near and I sprang the question.

'Do you have brassieres?'

I was not quite prepared for the consternation that followed. 'Hmm,' thinks I, 'That didn't work. '

'You know,' I tried again, 'Brassieres.'

I said it really slowly and just to help, I bounced a pair of imaginary air-tits with my hands at chest level, and looked inquisitively at the woman, who went a kind of red colour and disappeared.

That made me glum, and I was aware that Moira was feeling confused.

A few moments later the woman, apparently bearing me no lasting ill-will for having imaginary tits, returned, with an older woman whom I took to be the manageress.

'Good,' I thought, 'Five-star treatment.'

'We're looking for a brassiere,' I piped up cheerfully, to the newcomer, bouncing them again hopefully. 'For a baby, you know?'

If the first woman had looked surprised, both now looked horrified, bordering on outraged.

'A brassiere,' I intoned again, but left out the air-tits thing. That didn't seem to work at all.

The older woman adopted an air of decision and shook her head.

'Non. Pas de tout.'

'Oh...' I looked around. Well, maybe this was too much of a fashion shop.

'Do you know somewhere we could find one?'

'*Grande surface*,' replied the older woman, marginally forgiving. '*Castorama. Peut-etre.*'

Castorama is France's B&Q. That just didn't sound right. I shook my head.

There was an awkward moment while the five of us stood in silence, helpless. The first woman spoke up.

'There's a shop just along the road. You could try that. Just two blocks, on the corner.'

We thanked her and went on our way. Two blocks later we were standing in front of a charming, old fashioned *quincaillerie* – an ironmonger. I scratched my head. We had passed nothing that looked even vaguely like a maternity store. This was the right place, though. Two blocks, on the corner.

'We might as well try it,' I said to Moira, and we stepped within.

There was a woman behind the counter, and after the usual pleasantries, I asked again for a *brassiere*, for my wife. The woman looked at me, and then at my wife. 'A *brassiere*,' I repeated, and she sucked a tooth and frowned. The a light of recognition appeared on her face, and she exclaimed '*Ah, mais oui! Venez.*'

With that she bustled out from behind the counter and led the way to the dim recesses at the back of the shop.

There, grinning proudly, she showed me a small portable charcoal stove.

'No, no,' I said, and waved a hand at my very pregnant wife, 'For her baby.'

The woman's face darkened. '*Non, monsieur, pas de tout!*' and turned on her heel. We were left under no illusions that we should leave.

Once outside in the sunshine and increasing heat, Moira's exasperation became obvious. However, while occasionally absent-minded and sometimes even obtuse, I am generally not without resources. I spied, sitting on a bench, two young women with nursing age babies.

Chastened by my experiences thus far, I approached with caution, wife and child close by.

'Excuse me,' I asked. 'Do either of you speak English?'

Oh joy of joys! They both nodded and smiled. 'How can we help?'

'Well it's my wife. She needs a brassiere.'

'A *what?*'

Maybe they didn't speak the English so good after all. 'A brassiere'. I went for broke and did the air-tits thing. 'For the baby?'

For a moment there I thought it had all gone pear-shaped again, then one of the women's looks of consternation cleared. 'You mean a *bra?*'

Hallelujah. 'Yes!' I exclaimed. Further conversation was temporarily prevented, however, since the women were now in paroxysms. When at last they recovered composure, the first said, 'A bra. A maternity bra?'

'Yes.'

'Haha, that's a *soutien-gorge*. You've been asking for a brazier. You know, for cooking chestnuts.'

That would explain, I reflected, why the suggestion that it might be for a baby had caused such offence. The French may enjoy their frogs' legs and snails, but barbecued babies is strictly for *les Anglais*.

'Ahhh,' I said.

The women looked at each other, then at me and then at Moira. 'You stay here,' said our new friends, 'We'll sort this out.' And off they went, with the puzzled but relieved Moira, back to the very first shop; and there they did indeed find maternity bras.

The moral of this story is to beware the *faux ami*: the word that sounds French in English but means something totally different in France. There are lots of them.

Sandy Takes Down the Pine Tree

Sandy has always been a practical lad, as well as a smart one. He also has a thing about trees. He's a great tree-climber and I have often been welcomed home by the sight of his head sticking out of the top of one. He even went through a phase of sleeping up them. Unfortunately he fell out a lot so he stopped.

Anyway, behind our dream home in P'tit Moulin there is a nice courtyard. It's beautifully sunlit especially in the afternoons and early evenings. However, as is often the case here in Burgundy, the previous owner had planted one of his Christmas trees in the corner by the woodshed.

When we bought the house it was a sprightly young thing maybe seven or eight metres tall, and it didn't block the sun at any time. Fifteen years later, however, it stood well over twenty metres tall with a trunk sixty centimetres in diameter. This began to be a problem, because in those long balmy summer afternoons, which are, after all, a large part of the reason for being in France in the first place, it cast a giant shadow over the courtyard from about four. By six this was really quite unpleasant.

Well that's no good. I mean, six o'clock is when the bottles open and it's no fun at all to have to keep moving the table and chairs so that one can enjoy an *apero* in sunshine, is it? However the sheer size of the tree and the fact that it was on the edge of the property, within easy range of several roofs just waiting to be caved in by a ton or so of plummeting timber, stayed my chainsaw-wielding hand. The pine tree remained standing.

It was not without its benefits, that tree. I have always enjoyed the habit, after the *apero* hour, and then the relaxed meal that follows, of sitting out in my courtyard as the twilight falls. As the sky darkens, my friends the bats come out to play; many a happy hour have I spent watching them flit about. Well, that's what bats do, you know. The evening was when the pine tree came into its own, because in high summer, July and August, it was the home to a colony of cicadas, or *cigales* as they call them here.

It was always quite the pleasure, you know, a few glasses in, the sky a deep dark blue, magical bats flitting around and all with the sound of those cicadas...lovely.

Croutons and Cheese!

Then there came a time when, through unfortunate circumstance which will remain the subject of another book, since this one is meant to be very light-hearted and should be read semi-squiffed, we could not use our dream house for several years. Five in fact. When at last we returned, full of trepidation at what we might find, we were at first relieved. The roof was still there and no walls had fallen down. Inside, the spiders had been having a proper party to themselves and there was dust like Scottish snow blanketing everything; but all seemed well as I did a first inspection on the evening of our arrival.

'Mmmm,' thinks I, 'Perhaps a bottle of wine in the courtyard then.' We had a good cellar in those days; I am afraid I have drunk it all. With friends I hasten to add. Mostly.

So replete with said bottle, another *Nuits St Georges* 1993, I made my way from the *cave* to the courtyard via the barn, this being the quickest route. I opened the barn door and attempted to step outside. Unfortunately I was unable to do so, because of a wall of vegetation that reached high above my head. Well that was a bit awry.

'Mmm,' I thought again, somewhat less complacently. 'Maybe try the other way.' So back through the barn, into the house and all the way through that to the back door.

Same again. This door also opened inwards, but as soon as I tried to step outside, I hit a forest. Now feeling a little perturbed, I went upstairs to the dormer bedroom, where my worst fears were confirmed. It was by then almost dark, but I could still see that the courtyard, far from being an open space, had turned into a jungle. The vegetation appeared to be two metres tall at least. It was presided over by the sombre dark shadow of the pine tree, which looked to have put on another seven or so metres in height.

'Oh,' I thought. 'Well, I shall just have to drink this inside.' And so I did.

The next morning we rose late and a little stiff, because the journey from our home in Scotland to P'tit Moulin is just over a thousand miles. While Iain and Cait (the tribe had grown in the meantime) played around in the house, Sandy and I went to assess the damage in the courtyard.

All I could see, in the light of day, was green. Sandy, however, was bold. Taking a sickle, he hacked his way towards the centre of what had once been our courtyard. I followed him and took stock. This was not reassuring. It appeared that we now had at least a dozen sapling trees of various sorts, all growing where they shouldn't have been. What once had been shrubs were now two metres high, and in between all of this was chin-high savannah grass and nettles.

Over the next two days we attacked. I had left an electric chainsaw in the workshop. With that and a scythe we lopped, chopped, hacked and sawed until we once again had an open space, now with a huge pile of vegetation in the centre. I guess we were in the mood, so I had a good look at the pine tree. It had indeed grown prodigiously and had partly demolished the woodshed roof. At the same time it was pushing the courtyard wall over and alarming cracks had begun to appear. I shook my head. Something would have to be done.

'What about that while we're at it?' I asked Sandy, indicating the tree.

He frowned and I could see he was calculating. 'Won't it hit the roof?'

'Yes. So you'll have to climb it and drop it in sections.' I knew he couldn't resist that idea, and I was right.

Still, it was late and time to crack open the beers. We did sit out in the courtyard that night to watch the bats, but there were no cicadas. It made me feel better about what we were going to do.

The next day we began. Sandy was a strapping lad, fifteen years old by then, and more than fit for the job. There was no way I was going to let him try this with a chainsaw, electric or not, so he would have to do it with a bushman saw, which, happily, had a new blade. I tied a rope around his waist and showed him how to tie on to the trunk, and up the tree he disappeared.

A few minutes later, his head appeared near the top, wearing a huge grin and waving

Croutons and Cheese!

the bushman saw. 'Make sure you're properly tied on,' I called. Trees being lopped like this can whip viciously, so we were doing this by the book. I had no desire to see number two son catapulted through the air like a monkey off a stick – or for that matter, a cat off a tree.

Within a few minutes, the first section fell and I pulled it to the centre of courtyard. Sandy, using an axe, lopped the side branches off the tree as he descended, until he could saw the next section of trunk. Each of the branches he dropped I dragged to the pile, which was growing rapidly.

With about ten metres still standing, Sandy was beginning to struggle. He was a fit lad but it's hard work using a bushman with only one hand. He asked for a bigger axe and sent down a rope, and up it went. That helped for a while but the increasing thickness of the trunk was making it very hard going. With around seven metres to go he had to give up, gasping. 'It's no good. The weight of the tree is stopping me sawing.' He was apologetic.

I stepped back to consider. When I had I returned. 'Okay, come down. we'll drop the rest from here.' The tree would now at least not hit the barn, but it might demolish the old coal shed. But I thought if I cut it right and roped it, we could just about drop it between the coal shed and the one tree I wanted to keep. To do this I would have to climb onto the courtyard wall and cut the tree at about head height.

Sandy lashed a rope to the top of the remaining section and we led it off to the stump of a tree I had already chopped down, which happened to be in the right position. Sandy and Iain weren't strong enough to pull the tree in the direction I wanted themselves, but they could multiply their effort by pulling sideways. I used a lorryman's cinch (handy one that) to get the rope under real tension first, then told them what to do.

'When I shout "Timber!" you pull to the side as hard as you can, okay?'

Gleeful nods were received in return. Tree felling can be fun. I climbed the wall and delicately sawed out the dropping wedge, aiming the tree at the narrow space I wanted it to fall into. Then I gently made the felling cut, from the back side. The tree was out of balance because of the asymmetric lower branches, which were too thick for Sandy to cut and made it want to fall back towards my neighbour's wall. It was a tricky drop but I was confident if we could get it moving in the right direction all would be well. Then slowly I eased the blade in until I heard the first cracks.

'Timber! Pull, lads!' I yelled and made the final cut.

With the boys straining, I watched the top of the tree. It seemed undecided and I prepared to get out of the way by jumping down into the neighbour's garden. But then it gave up the struggle against the tension of the rope and the weakness I had introduced with the dropping wedge. The top described a gentle semicircle and then the last five metres crashed down exactly between the coal shed and the tree. We lost one small branch on the tree I wanted to keep but otherwise, a good job done.

Now we could have some real fun.

'Time for a bonfire,' I said. It was by then perhaps three in the afternoon, a warm still September day with a perfectly clear sky. A decent slathering of petrol and used engine oil and we had the mound of vegetation well alight.

Croutons and Cheese!

The thing about pine branches is that the needles burn very well even when green. The wax they contain and the pine resin itself are highly flammable. As soon as the branches we had already lopped took, the whole thing went up. It took another hour to saw off the remaining side branches from the felled trunk, which the lads piled on top of the bonfire. It was really spectacular. As well as burning very well, pine needles produce thick, choking mustard-yellow smoke, and soon a vertical column of it was rising hundreds of metres into the air.

Some time later I spoke to Charles, the schoolmaster. He had been in Nolay, ten kilometres away and had seen the smoke. Apparently everyone had.

'I knew it was coming from near here, so I was interested,' he said, 'Then, driving up the hill, I realised it was coming from right inside the village. I was pretty worried, but then I saw it was coming from your place.' He just shrugged, but I know what he had left unsaid – 'And you're nuts anyway.'

Sometimes a reputation like that comes in handy.

By the way, we had the famous P'tit Moulin flower-pot roasted chicken that night and very nice it was too, even if it tasted a bit more piney than usual. You can find the recipe in the first book.

The only thing I miss about that pine tree – and it doesn't make me regret dropping the damn thing – is that it was the home, in summer, to a chorus of cicadas.

Now the cicada, known in French as *cigale,* makes a delightful noise somewhere between a buzz and a chirp. It is a part of the insect's sexual behaviour, making it even more romantic. The cicada has been adopted by Provence as some sort of regional emblem, which led to a tricky situation one evening.

I was at dinner with a neighbour who spends a lot of her time in the South, and affects a southern origin, although she actually comes from Rennes. I happened to mention the cicadas, and she was, to put it mildly, offended that I could even dare to suggest that these quintessentially Provençal beasties could exist anywhere north of Orléans. She then proceeded to the crazy-*rosbif*-doesn't-have-a-clue-what-he's-talking-about attitude so beloved of the French when challenged by an Anglophone.

It being polite company I bit my tongue, but the next morning I hit Google. So, lest you find yourself in the same position, cicadas are indeed known far north of Provence. They are indigenous throughout France, including Alsace and there are even colonies in Holland, which no-one would pretend was cosy in winter. Yet more amazingly, perhaps, there is a species that lives in England, the New Forest Cicada; however we rather imagine they must have got lost at some time in the distant past.

Anyway, there was no sign of the P'tit Moulin cicadas this summer, but apparently they can live underground as larvae for up to seventeen years before hatching, when the conditions are right. So maybe the little dears will forgive me and come back.

Flaming Old Daimler

For some reason that I have never been able to fathom, things happen to me that just don't seem to happen to other people. Take my 1979 Daimler Sovereign Van den Plas for example. This is an extremely rare beast, by the way. It has the 4.2 litre straight-six XK motor, while most of this model were fitted with the 5.3 litre vee-twelve. Just so you know.

Anyway, at the time I was living in Scotland and had several lock-ups around the place, all filled with various forms of classic automobilia, something which I regarded as entirely normal. Apart from one, these were council lockups that had been rented by friends who had no present need of them. Still, they didn't want to let them go, just to be on the safe side. So my friends were happy to sublet them to me, in order to make a few shekels on the side while keeping the lockup.

Unfortunately, the Cooncil had other ideas and all of a sudden, three of these arrangements were threatened. Cooncil lockups could not be sublet, apparently. I imagine the Cooncil had its own good reasons for this but the upshot was inconvenient to say the least, because it meant that three Jaguars in various stages of decomposition were now homeless.

The best of these by far was the Daimler and indeed, I used it regularly as a summer car. It even had an MoT test certificate that I had not had to bribe the tester to get. The other two were not so blessed, however. So a decision, rational in every last detail was taken: I would sell the XJS (hairdresser express) and the nice but rusty manual-shift Series Three XJ6 I had been planning to have the gearbox out of, for scrap. Then I would take the Daimler to France, where I had a nice, big, empty garage. We were planning a month in the sun anyway so Moira would drive down in the estate car with the kids and dogs and I would drive the Daimler, wrap her up all cosy and warm, and then leave her there as a holiday car.

This was after I had met the nice gent with the partially-absent Fiat X-19 as described in the first book; I learn as I go along, you know. I could present the Daimler for its *Contrôle Technique* every summer and if it failed, so what? Two months of legal driving to fix it. Or I could not bother with any of that and just drive it on UK plates, since no-one ever checks the papers and anyway they're in English. (Since this is one of the very few advantages a Scot has that derive from the 'union' with

Perfidious Albion, one would be foolish not to use it, *n'est-ce pas?*)

It was a flawless plan, obviously.

The first indication that there might have been a leak (ho ho) in it was when we boarded *'le Tunnel'*. For those who might not be familiar with this aberration, instead of actually driving through the tunnel, you drive your car onto a special train and that goes through. All you have to do is sit there and not have any view to enjoy.

Anyway, I duly drove onto the train and waited. And waited. And waited. There we were, all set to go, when the train didn't.

Eventually it began to look as though we would not be going anywhere at all. Just then, along came a young man who said we had to clear the compartment. He did not explain why, just that we had to do it at once. It seemed an odd request, but one complies, doesn't one?

Once all the passengers were in the next compartment, the doors were sealed and a big flashy red light went on over them. This did not look so good. What on earth could be the problem?

It turned out that the trains' sensors had detected a whiff of petrol, but they did not know where from. I thought nothing of it. After all, the Daimler had a nice new MoT, didn't it? So I chatted with Calum and waited. Eventually, after 45 minutes or so, along came the nice person again, this time carrying a strange box with a probe on it, which my experience with petro-chemical industry clients told me was a 'sniffer'. The chap duly asked who owned the Daimler.

That was a little personal, but I indicated that I was the responsible party, and at once every other eye, about forty or so, swivelled onto me. Our man informed me that the faint whiff of petrol was coming from my car.

Well, anyone familiar with old Jags knows that is not in itself either very unusual or all that scary, but anyway. And it did have a nice new MoT, which I produced with a flourish.

There was a hiatus, during which I heard mutterings that the Daimler should be de-trained. However, our position meant that the entire carriage would have to be emptied. I felt confident and in due course, sure enough and after much debate by walkie-talkie, it was decided that the train would proceed. However, the passengers would have to remain where they were with the 'blast-doors' (seemed excessive) closed until we got to the other side of 'The Sleeve'. I was happy with this as I knew Moira, who had mysteriously been put on another train – which was long since departed and arrived by then – would be waiting and worrying.

We proceeded. I was aware that I was getting filthy looks from one character who was complaining that he had missed his 'vital meeting' in Brussels and that I should have been left behind. I applied my dear Auntie Ruth's maxim, and thought 'fuckim'. He wasn't nearly scary enough to give further consideration and if it were so important, then he should have gone the night before and stayed over.

We duly arrived at Calais and there was Moira, along with the rest of the brood, waiting indeed. It was getting on that way, so we opted to have lunch before continuing and then stop at Rheims for the night. (You know, the place that sounds like a bad cold.)

It was on the way there that the forewarned became the fact.

I have to say that I have no fondness for the area of France around Arras. This is not because it was utterly flattened by the heinous *Bosch* – twice – and reconstructed, giving everywhere a slightly – dare I say it – *ersatz* allure. No, it is because if anything bad is going to happen on my journey between our dream home in P'tit Moulin and my hieland hame (actually I am a Lowland Scot but you get the drift) then it always, always seems to happen at Arras. I think there's a French bogeyman there that has it in for me. I have even gone round the other side of Paris – without incident – many times to avoid the damn place. Not that I'm superstitious or anything.

Well it was just on that stretch of *autoroute* where if it's going to happen it will, that it happened.

Just after pulling out into the third lane to pass one of Norbert Dentressangle's bright red lorries, there was a loud thump as if I had hit someone. Immediately (I am not exaggerating) the passenger cabin filled with evil-smelling, thick smoke. It was a scary moment.

We were doing around 80 mph at the time and I snapped to Calum 'Undo your seat belt. When we stop, jump!' I knew there was a *sortie* – or exit ramp if you prefer – just blocked from my view by the artic I was overtaking. In front or behind? No time to debate, in front. I decked the throttle, the car dropped a gear and surged forward, and as I passed the truck, I pulled hard right, shot across his bows, between two other cars and up the ramp.

As soon as we were off the *autoroute* I killed the ignition and coasted – well, still doing a fair belt – up the slip and pulled over, screeching to a halt amongst gravel and whatnot. Very *Starsky and Hutch*.

'*Out!*' I yelled and Calum bailed while I did the same – but not before I had popped the bonnet latch. I remain cool under pressure, you know.

Now the thing with fire is it has logic. I have too, though it may not always be obvious. Anyway, fire is a fluid. You should remember this. It also needs fuel and oxygen. I knew that when I killed the ignition I had cut the fuel pump. As soon as I was out of the car – in less than a second or so – I had pulled the bonnet safety latch and thrown it open.

And yes there was fire.

The car did not have an extinguisher – these days I always carry one – but there were blankets in the back seat. I quickly retrieved one and threw it over the engine. As I did so, Moira pulled up behind. I didn't take time to remark on this but I was aware that she had jumped out of her car and was ushering Calum to safety while casting very troubled glances in my direction. Meantime a friend, Dave Renwick, who had come along for the ride, had also jumped out of her car and was emptying a can of Coke onto the blanket. This I regarded as very creative thinking.

I was even more impressed when he asked 'Do you want me to piss on it?'

I just laughed. The fire was out. After the fuel pump was cut only the hoses for the aircon system were actually burning and oxygen starvation soon had that fire out too. There was a small problem under the dash, which was smoking badly, but removing two screws had me inside that and I quickly ripped out the foam plastic that was smouldering there. In less than three or four minutes from that initial, heart-stopping thump, the fire was completely out and no-one had been burned.

Moira hove into view and I gave her a squeeze and a kiss.

'Idiot,' she said. 'Are you okay?'

'Yes, I'm fine,' I replied. I smiled at her. 'You acted quickly, to get in here after me. You must have realised something was wrong.'

She just stared at me, aghast. 'Didn't you look in your mirror?'

'No, I was concentrating on where we were going. There was too much smoke in there to see anything, anyway.'

She shook her head in amazement. 'Rod...there was a sheet of flame at least thirty feet long coming from under the car. Notice? Are you kidding?'

'Really?'

Croutons and Cheese!

'Yes. Christ alone knows what that trucker you carved up must have thought. Why didn't you go behind him? You should have seen his face.'

'Because you were in front and I needed to let you know I had a problem...And it worked.'

Dee and the Birthday Cake

Time for some doggie tales (ho ho.)

Avid readers of the first volume in this deliberately idiosyncratic memoir will remember the moment when I found myself looking down the barrel of a customs officer's weapon, erm, firearm. This was a result of my car smelling like the canine equivalent of a whore's boudoir, as my Auntie Ruth says. Well, the particular specimen of *Canis* that was the cause of all that had a chequered history indeed, as I shall soon reveal.

But first, I thought I would take a moment just to mention, to some readers who avail themselves of free downloads and don't have the courtesy to shut their traps, that if I care to write about politics, the Flying Spaghetti Monster or Uncle Tom Cobbley, then it's my affair. If, on the other hand, you are the sort of decent cove that understands and appreciates the use of hyperbole, licence and invention, then read on and please feel free to contact me through my blog at http://rodfleming.com. You'll find that I am a singularly personable chap. And just to show you that I am a champion at compromise, all the technical stuff that I was going to put in this book will now appear in a separate one – leaving more space here for fun.

Where was I? Oh yes, the canine equivalent of Mata Hari. Her name was Dee and she had joined our happy little troop a couple of years before we went to France. Quite why my wife, the lovely Moira, had found it necessary to visit the dog pounds in all the major Scottish cities to find her was never clear to me.

The first inkling I had of her existence was when I came home from work one evening, went to the bathroom to unload the couple of beers I had had on the way, and a very deep growl came from behind me. Turning in surprise – our other dog, Holly, didn't sound a bit like that – there she was. With my wife, looking a little sheepish, behind her. Maybe the fact that I still had my willie in my hand had something to do with that, mark you.

Anyway, as far as we could make out, Dee was an Alsatian (oh all right, GSD) and greyhound cross, a kind of lurcher. She looked like an

Croutons and Cheese!

Alsatian but taller and thinner and with a finer head and HUGE ears. We fell in love instantly. (Even though she was nominally Moira's dog.)

Dee was from Glasgow and it is possible that this may explain a few things. As well as which, Dee had, as her teacher, Holly. Now the latter was a recidivist reprobate of the worst order, given to all sorts of mischief and worse, training Dee in them. She came from Dundee, which definitely explains a lot.

The keystone of Holly's arch of crime was that she would encourage Dee to do something really BAD – and I don't mean just bad – and at the last moment vamoose. She would curl up in her basket with one eye open, looking innocently at the human who had just arrived to see Dee standing over the disembowelled remains of yet another teddy bear. You get my drift about that one's character.

The result of her training in the Holly School of Horrible Dogness was that Dee, being a good Glaswegian, became an even more legendary troublemaker than her mentor. As the reader is about to see, illustrated by a few delightfully crafted memories of her.

Now Dee was a fairly big dog but she had a remarkable talent for getting through small spaces. In our dream pile in France there was once a very low back door into the courtyard. This was the one whose lintel I had near as dammit brained myself on several times, as regular readers might recall.

While that door has long since been consigned to the ceremonial bonfire and replaced with one tall enough for a modern *Homo sapiens,* at the time of which I write it was still in place. It was half-glazed, with nine panes of glass, each around nine inches square. One of these was broken – not uncommon in that house – and had been repaired in the time-honoured fashion, with a piece of crumpled newspaper stuffed in the hole.

This was at the height of the rejuvenated *Thunderbirds* craze, the puppet series from the 1960s that I, as a lad, had been a big fan of. Now my own son was crazy about all things Thunderbird and I had even been able to give him several original merchandising toys from the era, including my Dinky Toys pink FAB 1. (Fans will remember. It was Lady Penelope's Rolls.) Well, for Calum's birthday something special had to be done and since we, as parents, were into the 'theme cake' approach, or at least Moira was, she determined to make a big green Thunderbird Two complete with Virgil.

The making of this culinary work of art took all morning on the big day, while I was charged with making sure that Calum did not catch a glimpse of what was going on. Just as well, as it happened. About 11:30 Moira pronounced herself satisfied with the cake diorama she had created. (Did I mention that she is a sculptor? Well, she is.) The Thunderbird Two was truly magnificent and it had been set on a base with little Virgil beside. Lovely.

We needed to put it somewhere cool and the whole lot was much too big for the fridge, so we put it, instead, in the back room, which was then still being refurbished. Moira put some newspapers down on the table in there and closed and bolted the door to the kitchen. This was so that the dogs couldn't get in, you see? The back door – that low one with the small panes of glass, you recall – was similarly made lockfast, as they say, and we set to preparing for the onslaught of kids, Calum's friends, who were due to arrive at three.

The *grande salle* duly decked out with bunting, the table – actually three put together – set and readied, and the main course – spaghetti if I recall – under way, I went through the back room to refill a log basket. Calum's birthday is in November and it can get a bit chilly in the hilly fastness of the Arrière-côte.

Imagine my horror, consternation and dismay then, as I laid my boggled eyes on the table where had been placed the magnificent Thunderbird Two. All was awry and the cake was on the floor. Its nose-cone had been eaten, and of poor Virgil there remained only the boots.

I actually screamed.

Naturally, a search was on for the culprit, but there was no sign. How could this be? A cat? But no, cats don't have teeth that big, well, not in P'tit Moulin. I hope not, anyway. That was when I spotted the evidence. The glass in the one pane that was broken was now entirely missing and bits were scattered on the floor. Close examination revealed the truth. Some of Dee's distinctive salt-and-pepper grey hairs were caught in the woodwork around the hole.

Moira, who had arrived by

then, came over. Her face was black with rage.

'Oh, that *bloody dog!*' she snapped. I was reminded, not for the first time, that Dee was *my* dog, whenever she was bad. Which seemed strange, since, as attentive readers will have spotted, I didn't drive all the way from Dunbar to Glasgow dog pound to find her. But we shall, as they say where I come from, just let that fly stick to the wall.

Of the bitch (neutered) herself there was no sign; she had clearly made good her escape the same way as she had got in, there being no other entrance or exit.

No time was wasted in a futile attempt to catch and punish the perpetrator of this atrocity, but a party had to have a cake.

Did I mention that Moira is a sculptor? Yes, well so am I. 'There must be something we can do,' I mused. 'You look after Calum and keep him out of the way, I'll fix this.'

I fetched a little hardboard and quickly made up a background. I stuck paper on it and then painted in a sky and clouds, and a pretty decent (I thought) sketch of the *Thunderbirds* logo in yellow and red. I believe the typeface might be Playbill, by the way. This I fixed to a baseboard. There was enough of the wrecked 'ground' where Virgil had been standing to save, and this was put in place. The old nose-cone of Thunderbird Two – now inside that dog – was trimmed off smooth and with a bit of art the cake was mounted so that it looked as if it were taking off into the sky.

And thus was the day saved. I really don't think Calum even noticed. But that dog was in the bad books for a week.

Dee's remarkable ability to elongate herself and squeeze through holes that were smaller than she was had other consequences. We had, one weekend, planned a great roast. This was in the early days before I had remodelled the kitchen. For reasons that I confess, distance of time and cerebral addling due to red wine have obscured, the roast was placed in a heavy cast-iron pot to relax – a *marmite* in France, so now you know where the name comes from. The *marmite* was placed on the end of the kitchen table.

We had to nip into the local supermarket for some last minute essentials – another way of saying that we had scoffed the wine we already bought the night before. It's only six kilometres to the shop and we reckoned to be away half an hour.

Dee, at this time, slept under the kitchen table, which was a vast and profoundly characterless oak horror that had been crudely painted white by the pervious owner, who had then stuck linoleum tiles on the top. He did have a way with style, that one. Anyway the damn thing weighed a good 60kg if not more and was a struggle for two my size to shift – and I am not petite, like.

We had an arrangement whereby the dog or dogs could be tied to the leg of this piece of architecture. We reasoned that if it were a struggle for me to shift it, they'd have no chance. Since we were only going out for half an hour, and the weather was foul, we tied Dee up there rather than put her out. She was sleeping in her basket there and looked so innocent (I know, I know).

Now this table was two metres long. The *marmite* was at the far end of the table from where Dee was tied, on a leash that was only 1.5 metres long. No problem, huh? And furthermore, the cast-iron *marmite* had an equally no-nonsense cast-iron lid, which was tricky to remove even for a human with actual digits and opposable thumbs.

So with all that in place, there was no problem, right?

We went to the supermarket and stocked up with vino collapso. When we got back, only a half an hour later, a quick glance confirmed: the *marmite* was still there with no sign of violation, and Dee was still happily tied up. Maybe a little too happily.

I do not recall what the first course at our repast was. Perhaps paté. Moira is good at making patés and often did, back then. Then the moment came to begin the roast, so off she went through to the kitchen to fetch it (we were being posh and using the *grande salle*) and the next thing I heard was a loud shriek.

Thinking some near-fatal accident must have occurred or Jack the Ripper had rematerialised in P'tit Moulin, I rushed through to find Moira, with the *marmite* cover in her hands, looking aghast into it. Where there was sign of neither roast nor gravy. It was completely empty and spotless.

No wonder that damn mutt was looking so happy!

We measured the leash. It was still only 1.5 metres long. There was no way Dee could have reached that pot, but she clearly must have, and not only that, lifted the lid, removed the meat, licked out the pot and dropped the lid back on. Without leaving a trace of her thievery. For weeks after we would stop, measure the leash, shake our heads and wonder. Was this some weird phantom we had inherited from Glasgow

Croutons and Cheese!

Dog Pound? Or just the most talented thief in history? She made the Pink Panther look inept.

Well that was that. We had frozen pizzas for lunch and learned a lesson about the shape-shifting abilities, not to mention downright sneakiness, of certain individuals of the canine persuasion.

Dee's canine kleptomania didn't always work against us. Once, in Scotland, before we went to France, it happened that we had no Christmas cake. We had everything else, including a Sicilian gateau in the form of a swan with several cygnets following (I kid you not) courtesy of the excellent *Pasticceria Siciliana* in Edinburgh's Albert Street. But no cake.

I have always had a horror of those traditional black Christmas cakes that weigh on your stomach like a lump of lead. But my mother – the one I nearly lost in the SNCF, you remember (not that I ever had more than one) – was coming to visit and Mum did like her traditional Christmas cake.

The absence of a cake to appease my mother was only discovered on Christmas Eve, for the simple reason that Moira had assumed I would buy one and I had assumed she would bake one. Fairly standard for marital communications I believe. Anyway we were left with a problem, because then we lived in Dunbar, the local bakeries were closed and I was not about to take another commute into Edinburgh.

'Stuff it,' I said. (Well I probably said something considerably more firm, but I understand some readers are sensitive to that sort of thing. Not you, of course.) 'She'll just have to have something else with her damn sherry.' And with that I cracked the first bottle, settling the argument before it began – no driving.

Nevertheless I knew from my mother's reaction that she was disappointed not to see a traditional Christmas cake on the table and this disappointment was going to percolate the festivities like a dark miasma.

'Damn Christmas cake,' growled Moira while we were in the kitchen.

'You hate it,' I pointed out.

'Yes, but your mother is going to sulk.'

It was true, but what could be done? There was no solution that I could see except to have the sherry without the cake.

'I suppose we could have shortie.'

'You know she hates it.'

'Stuff it then, she'll just have to sulk.'

Just at that moment, however, something odd happened. Our dogs were used to coming and going pretty much as they pleased and the front door was usually left open so that they could. I looked out into the hallway, and there was Dee, with something large and black clamped in her jowls, coming up the stairs. She had an uncommonly self-satisfied air about her – which is really saying something for that mutt.

'What the blazes is that?' We looked at each other quizzically.

'I have no idea.'

We followed Dee into the living room where she had settled down in front of the fire with her trophy.

'My God,' I said. 'It's a Christmas cake.'

'What? How…'

'It is, look,' I said, approaching the hairy one, who was grinning at me and lolling her tongue. She was always a pleasant character and she let me take the cake without too much fuss. She'd eaten a bit of it but most was intact, well, apart from a few tooth-marks.

'Where do you suppose she got that from?' asked Moira.

At that moment my mother appeared, all dressed up like she was going to the Ritz. She laughed. 'Your grandmother always used to put the cake on the window sill to cool. I bet that's what happened. Dee just took it.'

'Yes, but whose window?'

I looked out over Dunbar; it was already dark and a miserable wind tugged at the windows. It was not encouraging. There were over a hundred houses clearly visible, further down the hill, all festively lit, any one of which might be the home of the mystery cake-baker. I did not relish the idea of wandering about for hours finding out which. And what if the owner accused me of theft? Heavens I might be arrested and spend Christmas in the slammer. No thanks.

'You can't take that back,' laughed Moira. 'It's been mauled. Look at it.'

'True,' I replied, thankful for an excuse to do nothing. That sherry was rather nice.

'So…let her finish it?'

'Oh no,' quoth my partner in crime. 'I have some marzipan and icing. We'll just trim off the slobbery bits and eat it.'

'Good idea.'

So my mother had cake with her sherry and pronounced it a proper

Croutons and Cheese!

Christmas after all. She even approved my trifle.

When we came to return to the Sceptred Isle (well you know what I mean) after our first sojourn in France, we had a problem called two dogs and a cat. Dee had struck up a whirlwind dogmance with Luc *le Taxis*, Antoine *le Potier*'s brother, however, and the sentiment was reciprocated. So when I explained to Luc that Dee would have to spend six months in quarantine – this being before pet passports – he needed no second asking and with tears in my eyes I handed her over to her new-found love.

It was none of Luc's fault, but a few years after that, when Dee was eight, she got out of the house one afternoon. When Luc arrived home and parked on the other side of the road, she ran to greet him – and was struck by a lorry. Her spine was broken and she had to be euthenased.

I cried when I heard the news, as I am sure Luc had. For all her faults and despite a criminal record as long as my arm, Dee was a very special dog who touched the heart of everyone who knew her.

Poor Sweepie

On our second sojourn in France we were joined by our two greyhounds, Sweepie and Benji. Sweepie had been a successful racer in her youth but like so many had been retired at four years of age. The repeated strain of racing begins to damage the skeleton after a while and so, when greyhound racing was popular, there were always retired greyhounds free to good homes. Whether this remains the case I do not know.

When we returned from France to Scotland after our first two-year stay we were without dogs, so Moira lost no time in adopting; which is how Sweepie came to be with us.

By the time we were ready to return to Scotland after our second two-year stay in France, Sweepie was already twelve years old and this presented a problem. By that time the Pet Passport scheme had been adopted throughout Europe. The United Kingdom had been dragged squealing into the 20th century (not a mistake) and had been obliged to implement it by those nice chaps in Brussels. This process involved having the dogs vaccinated against rabies, undergoing a blood test to confirm the presence of antibodies and then being electronically chipped to confirm their status. The problem was that in older dogs – and for that matter humans – the immune system may not respond properly to the vaccination, with the result that the antibodies do not form as they should.

Benji was a mere stripling of four and his test came back positive; but there was a problem with Sweepie. Her antibody count was practically zero. We elected to have another rabies vaccine, and then see what would happen. The vet was confident that the second shot would kick-start the production of antibodies. He said he'd seen this before in an older dog.

In those days I was the official photographer for the Perrier *Pick of the Fringe* comedy talent competition at the Edinburgh Festival Fringe every year. It was a really well paid gig and I used to combine it with a trip to Scotland to see my mother, whose health was beginning to worry me.

I took a three week trip to Scotland, flying out from the little airport at Dijon. After a few days back I got the first bad news: Sweepie had failed her second blood test. This was a dilemma, but we still had over eight months before we planned to return to Scotland, so I was not too worried. Even if the vaccination simply would not take and she could not have a Pet Passport, Sweepie was a very lovable dog and there was no shortage of good homes on offer for her. It would be sad to have to leave her, but she was an old dog and the upheaval of moving would be stressful for her.

The second piece of bad news came the day after the Perrier, while I was sending the pictures out to the media. Sweepie – like all greyhounds an inveterate thief – had managed to get into a bin where there had been a cooked chicken carcass. She had eaten the bones and one of them must have torn the inside of her throat, because it was drastically swollen. Moira had had to take her to the vet on an emergency call the night before, and she was still at the surgery under sedation and heavy antibiotics.

By the time I got back, Sweepie was home and was, as ever, delighted to see me. She was really a lovely dog. But I could see that all was not well. She was feeble, is the only way I could describe it. She had lost weight – and greyhounds have very little fat so they can't afford to do that – and she was shaky on her legs, something she had never been.

I was worried about my old friend.

Two weeks later my fears were realised. I came down to the kitchen one morning and was horrified by the noise I heard. Sweepie's throat had swollen up again. She was lying in her basket and the awful noise was her breathing. Her windpipe was clearly almost completely blocked and breathing was nearly impossible for her. She was lying in her basket and had not got up. Her eyes told the tale of her pain and confusion.

I woke Moira and together we lifted Sweepie into the car. I took her to the vet alone, with a heavy heart.

The nice vet at Épinac opened up for me although it was a Sunday and I knew from his face that things were bad. After a quick examination, during which there was a fair bit of sucking of veterinarial teeth, he nodded and looked at me.

'I can do a tracheotomy and relieve the breathing problem. But the throat is badly damaged. I would have to operate.'

I nodded, but this was an honest French country vet.

'Monsieur, there is really not much chance that the operation would be successful. Her immune system has collapsed completely. I can try, but...' He shrugged. I knew what he meant.

'It would be kinder to euthenase her?'

'It's your decision, monsieur,' he replied diplomatically, but his meaning was clear. 'I will leave you for a moment while you decide.'

It took no effort. When we accept responsibility for the lives of our pets, we also take responsibility for their deaths. Sweepie had been getting progressively weaker ever since I returned, more and more shaky on her legs. She had that constant look of pain and confusion and she was still losing weight because she would not eat – probably because it hurt. We were feeding her the smoothest and richest, tastiest food we could, but even that was not enough to tempt her.

I held her in my arms. Despite the shallowness of her breathing and the fact that she was obviously in pain, she trusted me to do the right thing. I had no choice.

When the vet came back in, I just nodded and he prepared the syringe. I cried all the way back to our house in P'tit Moulin.

Later, after Benji passed, again euthanased, this time because of a chronic back problem that meant he could barely stand up, I learned something.

Poor Benji's great delight was to walk and he would do so all day. He especially loved the beach and no matter how lazy he was being, just saying 'beach, beach', would have him up and beside the door, tail wagging. During his last winter he slipped on some ice outside the front door and injured his back. Over the next few months it got worse, until he could hardly get off his sofa. The vet said to walk him, so I tried; but one day in spring, I took him to the beach and it was sheer misery for him. He looked at me when we got back to the car and I knew what I had to do.

A wise Thai friend of mine said to me once, 'We are responsible for those we tame.' She is right. Being a pet owner carries a heavy responsibility. Since Benji, I have not had another dog. Moira still does, but I have not. I tell people and myself that this is because I travel too much now and it would be impossible to keep a dog.

But this is only a partial truth. The other part is that I do not wish to have that responsibility again. It hurts too much.

Les Quattors Juillets

P'tit Moulin used to have a legendary reputation in the matter of Bastille Day *spectacles*. Seriously, it was known throughout the Arrière-côte as one of the best in the area. No-one knew exactly when the tradition had begun, but generations before, the local schoolmaster had started presenting a little show with the schoolchildren. Like Topsy it growed and growed. Soon the parents became involved. As the first crop of children grew up, they still took part. Then their kids did too. By the time we arrived in P'tit Moulin the event involved sixty or more people aged from five to seventy as stars, 'go-fors', propmakers and backstage helpers. Most of them had been participating all their lives.

The *spectacles* themselves took the form of a series of set-piece dances performed to popular music, with a fair bit of lip-synch miming. Good traditional French country stuff.

The event itself would begin the evening before, on the 13th of July, when the villagers, including the performers in costume, would gather in the square in front of our house. Tricolour lanterns were handed out to the crowd and lit and then, after a few words from the mayor, there was a processions through the village. As well as the performers and spectators there were floats – tractor trailers – decorated with scenes from the *spectacle*.

The procession wound its way through the village before arriving at the old station where Kiki *la Gare* lived. The old platform was used as the stage, and the *salle des fêtes*, which is opposite, was opened.

First – this being France – there was a *vin d'honneur*, a toast, of red or white wine or *kir*. After this and the usual pressing of palms, the audience went outside to sit on the benches and chairs there to watch *le spectacle*. It really was a credit to the hard work of the schoolteacher and the organising committee. Some ten or so set pieces, all in costume, with music, is no easy feat to put together and it was always a delight to see the successful result of all the effort.

After the show, the gathered company would eat and, of course, drink. Some did this more seriously than others.

The next morning everyone would gather outside our house again for the roll of honour, the naming of the fallen. The veterans – a dwindling number – would be at the front of the crowd. Two of the younger men would read off the names of the fallen which were inscribed on the War Memorial.

Each name was called in turn, and the words *'mort pour la France'* in reply. Once the roll was called, the *Fanfare d'Épinac*, an orchestra of delight if ever there was one, would lead *'La Marseillaise'*. After that there would not be a dry eye in the crowd.

Then the mayor would make a short speech thanking everyone for their efforts, and the assembly would proceed – this time without lanterns – down to the old station, where the events of the night before would be repeated, at a slightly more leisurely pace.

After the *spectacle*, performed exactly as before, everyone, including the performers, could relax. That was something they took very seriously.

In those long-gone, halcyon days, there would be perhaps four or five hundred people at the *Quattors Juillet*. Most had some connection with the village but many now lived far away, in Lyon or Paris or Marseilles. Yet they would always come back to their roots. As well as these there would be those who lived in the area and knew that the P'tit Moulin *Quattors* was one of the best and so they would show up too.

(As a matter of fact, the *Quattors Juillet* festivities were taken so seriously that they were spread over several days with different villages holding their event on each, in order to attract the greatest possible number of patrons. This made it possible to celebrate the Revolution – with the associated drinking and eating – over three or more days. Almost as good as New Year in Scotland used to be.)

In order to raise money and maximise the attraction, the village organised a raft of other activities. There was a bar, a *crêpe* stall, a barbecue, and other cooked food stalls, all set up under a huge awning. Another awning outside the *salle des fêtes* protected the tables where the serious eating and drinking was done. The Festival of *Quattors Juillet* was a great money-spinner for the commune, raising significant cash that was spent helping the elderly in the village.

The volunteer fire brigade – now defunct – organised the entertainment. There was a coconut shy, one of those eat-the-pancake-off-a-string things, an archery stand, ten-pin bowling (true; we have a permanent bowling alley all built of concrete) but most spectacular of all was the fishing pond.

This was a square pool formed from straw bales with a sheet of black plastic inside, held in place with stones around the outside. The pool was then filled with water (from the fire engine) and stocked with trout. For ten francs you got a rudimentary fishing rod to which was attached a metre and a half of nylon line and a hook. The bait was a grain of maize (cooked) placed on the hook. You had till one of the thoroughly befuddled fish actually took said bait or the corn fell off.

I never actually saw anyone catch a trout, but I am told it did happen.

*Le Fanfare d'*Épinac was on hand throughout the afternoon and periodically launched into stirring, if a little shaky, renditions of what I am sure were famous French tunes.

The drinking and eating (and attempting to catch trout) continued until the evening, when there would be a dinner dance inside the Salle de *Fête* for those still able to take part, usually with a traditional accordionist. Around midnight the crowds began to disperse and by one there would only be a diehard or two left.

In 2002 we had four children in school in P'tit Moulin and naturally they took part in *le spectacle*. The theme that year was The Wild West, in a very French, Lucky Luke inspired style. Each of our children had costumes, which were partly made by the loyal parents, including us and partly by the committee. Many of the audience turned out in cowboy regalia too. I was the official photographer and it was a lot of fun.

Now this is France and the Fourteenth of July is at the hottest part of the hottest month. This can lead to mighty convectional thunderstorms. On one memorable year the rain was so torrential that the awnings collapsed. (That year, along with a few others, I used my 4x4 to ferry the elderly and mothers with children back to their homes.) On other occasions, sudden hailstorms would break out, sending everyone running for cover. But all in all, *Quattors Juillet* at P'tit Moulin was a day to look forward to and to remember.

Sadly, like much of rural France, P'tit Moulin has been hit by the curse of country areas across Europe: rural depopulation. This has meant that while the little village school remains open – at least for now

– this has only been possible because the school is now grouped with those in two other villages. The children are divided according to age and bussed to the appropriate school. P'tit Moulin now serves only the youngest; *Maternelle* and Primaries One and Two. While this means that at least we still have a school, there is no longer the continuity that made the old *spectacles* possible. There are no older children to help teach the young ones and, to be fair, the teachers now have other things to do than spend many extra hours working to prepare a *spectacle* in a village in which they do not live. 2011 was the last in the great tradition of *les spectacles de Quattors Juillet de P'tit Moulin*.

It is a sad loss indeed, but we were privileged to be a part of it.

Croutons and Cheese!

French Onion Soup! II

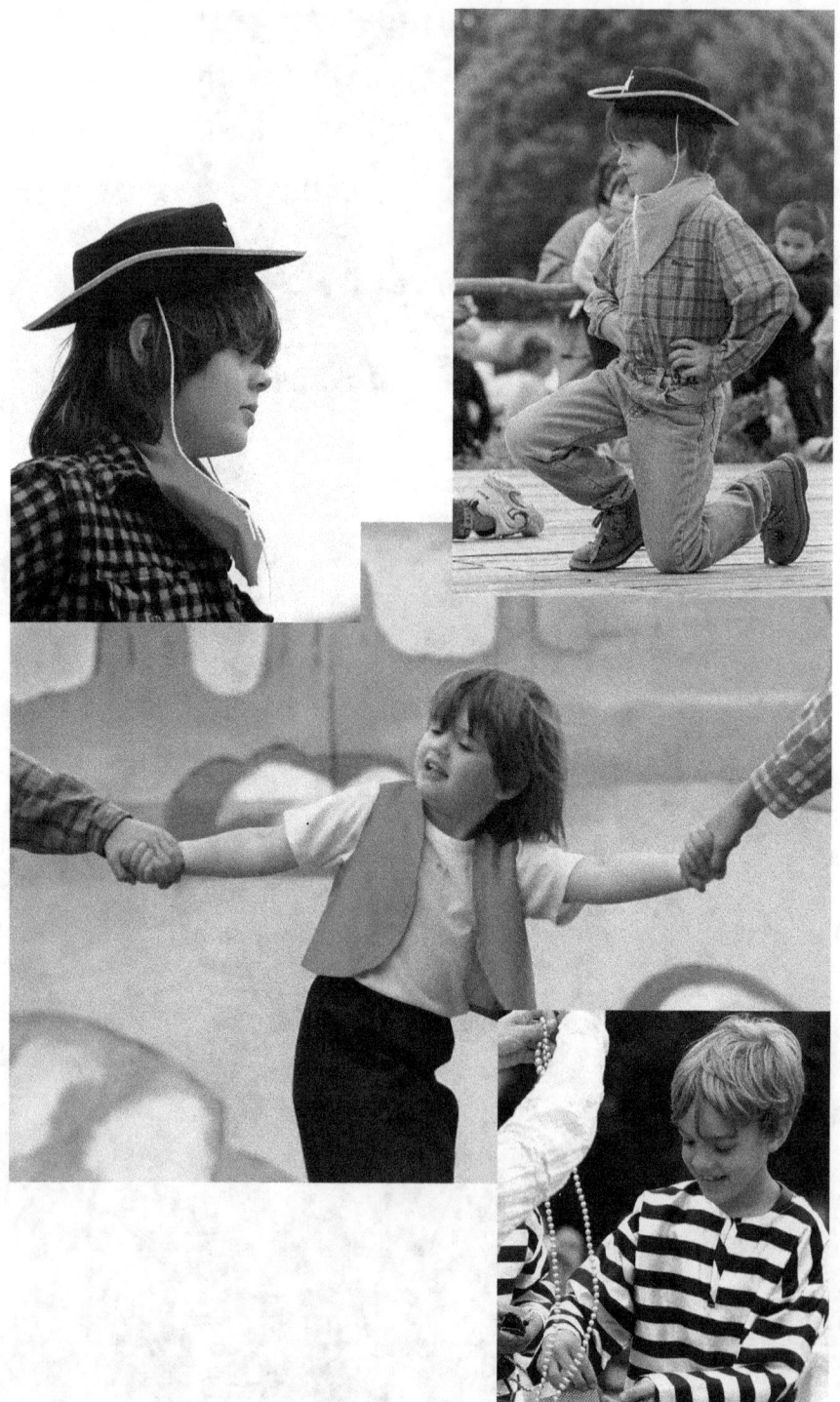

Croutons and Cheese!

French Onion Soup! II

The Woman Whose Car Would Not Start

There was an old woman of quaint hygiene who lived in a semi-derelict farm just on the outskirts of the village. She had once been stylish, judging by her clothes, but she had laid off keeping up-to-date a couple of decades beforehand. Her clothes were, while still elegant, now worn out. Country life does that to you. Trust me, I know. Given that she apparently never washed them (or herself) her clothes were quite striking in other ways too.

She and her husband – a cheery individual with the prominent red nose of the alcoholic and yellow *caporal* stains on his white moustache – were regular clients at *Chez Angèle* next door. Despite this, I have to say that I never really got to know them. She seemed rather distant though always polite, but her husband was completely incomprehensible. He spoke a ferocious patois, his dentures fitted only where they touched and he was perpetually three sheets to the wind.

They don't have alcoholism in France, you know.

Anyway, one morning – in those days the cafe trade started early – just before lunchtime, I became aware of a rather nasty smell in the house. No, not that kind. Petrol.

'Hmmm,' thinks I, 'Better investigate.' Now the crusty couple (he was certainly no cleaner than she) habitually parked right outside our front door, something which I didn't mind too much. After all, it was their village. But choking the house up with petrol fumes was a bit much even for a tolerant cove like me. And we were about to have lunch you know…I mean it doesn't do to fug the place up with noxious vapour at times like that. As I was constantly telling my children.

Outside the door, as usual, was the crusty couple's venerable Renault 11, a rather tasteful shade of duo-tone battleship grey and rust. Mr Crusty was in the passenger seat, his bleary and bloodshot eyes surveying all around him with the serenity of the serious drinker, while his good lady was trying to start the car.

It was not going well. There was enough petrol vapour to fill a tanker and the starter-motor had got to that slow chug that says battery failure is imminent. I was seriously hoping that Mr Crusty would not have a sudden desire to spark up a maize-paper *caporal* and blow us all into high heaven as the vapour exploded.

Well it happens that those old Renaults had a thing called an 'automatic starter' which would have been better named an 'automatic non-starter' for that was what it usually ensured. It was really just an automatic choke operated by a bimetallic strip. This meant that when the engine was cold the choke flap was closed to enrich the starting mixture. So far so good. When the engine was hot, the choke was held open by the bimetallic strip, delivering a weaker, running mixture to the hungry cylinders. So far so better.

Unfortunately (for the owner) if the engine were only partly warmed and then the car stopped, the bimetallic strip would cool and close the choke, but the engine still wanted a weak mixture. Not good at all and the joy of garage owners in the old days, because they got countless call-outs to start 'broken down cars' when actually the issue was simply that their engines were flooded because the choke was full on. Nice work while it lasted, hey?

There were several different hacks for getting round the problem and I volunteered my services. However, the good lady had her own ideas. She would like me, she indicated, to push her car down the hill. I realised that this would not work, but I played bonny; it was easy to push down the hill after all, not like pushing up it. I followed the car down the slope, enveloped in petrol vapour, till it came to a standstill at the bottom, which was inevitable.

'Now,' I explained, since her idea had not worked, 'Try this.' The crack was actually quite easy on the Renault, you just slowly pushed the accelerator pedal to the floor and held it there, then cranked it like billy-oh. Fortunately there was enough battery left to do that. The motor caught on about the fourth turn and wheezed into life while punting a dense fug of black smoke out the exhaust. A couple of revs and it was running clean again.

With grins all round, we said our farewells as she wove her way back to her farm.

The story had a nice ending though. Every year after that until in the end she died, the lady would bring me, harvested from her own trees, a huge basket of quinces. Lovely.

It's nice to be nice.

Kiki la Gare

Avid readers of the first book in this series, *French Onion Soup!* have already made the acquaintance of Kiki *la Gare*. While our first meeting with the estimable Kiki was, shall we say, a memorable experience, time proved that he was far from the terrifying troglodyte that he at first appeared to be.

Kiki was short, about 5'4". He had perhaps once been a little taller, but years and a spectacular hunch-back had reduced him in stature if not in character. He was swarthy of skin and smoked *caporal*. His habitual clothes were working men's blues and boots, which are worn with pride all over France. Well, at least they used to be. The sartorial revolution of the 1970s appears to have finally arrived, and men are even seen wearing jeans and checked shirts these days. The ensemble was topped off by the regulation Moulinard flat cap .

On the one occasion when he removed his cap in my presence, I was amazed to see, above the encircling short hair, a perfectly white, smooth bald pate. Since the rest of him was brown and gnarled as a walnut, this came as something of a surprise and it was all I could do not to stare. However, I was later to discover that this distinctive feature was typical of the men of the village.

We were to find that Kiki was a fine ambassador for P'tit Moulin and had many qualities, even if he did bear more than a passing resemblance to a goblin.

Kiki, it turned out, loved children. He had been married but his wife had died and his children, like so many others, had long since decamped to the big cities in search of work and a better life than P'tit Moulin could offer. The Arrière-côte is beautiful, but full of opportunity it is not and few these days look with relish on the life of a peasant farmer; who could blame them?

It was really through his love of children that we got to know him. Kiki *la Gare* lived, unsurprisingly, in *la Gare*, the old station building. The railway was long gone. It had been a narrow-gauge one, built in the 19th century to take coal from the mines in Épinac to the railhead at Pont d'Ouche, where it was loaded into barges to be shipped to Paris and Lyon. With the end of the coal-mines, the tracks had been lifted, but the buildings remained. The station at P'tit Moulin had been taken over by the commune and it is now rented out.

At the time of which I write (as they say) the only tenant in *la Gare* was Kiki, and nobody could remember quite when he had moved in; a long time before, in any case. With his family all gone he lived in one room on the round floor, which was, to put it mildly, extremely damp.

To keep himself warm, Kiki used a gas space-heater fuelled by butane, which came in those blue bottles. The trouble with these heaters is that for every litre of gas you burn, they produce a litre of water. This enters the atmosphere as water vapour and of course, ends up on the walls, condenses and makes them wet.

This was a vicious cycle with Kiki burning more and more gas in order to keep warm and his walls getting more and more damp and chilling the house. It meant that Kiki went through a lot of gas, and he used to walk up the hill to *Chez Angèle* and buy it there. (He could have saved a lot of effort by going to the shop for his gas, but Kiki was a creature of habit.) He trailed his bottle behind him in an old-fashioned shopping trolly.

Our house, as you know, is one of the most prominent in the village and it has a *banc*. Frequently I would find Kiki sitting on it, catching his breath – it really is a steep hill up to the house. After a while I began to go out and sit with him and even offered him coffee, which he always refused.

Kiki was actually very shy and rather ill at ease in adult company, but when surrounded by children he transformed. His eyes brightened and his sense of fun – not something that was usually too obvious – came out. He brought little presents for the boys, never very much but still much appreciated; sometimes clothes, or chocolates or toys.

After a while something remarkable happened: Kiki invited us for lunch. Now the import of this should be understood. In all the time we lived in and visited P'tit Moulin, Kiki was the only native of the village who has *ever* invited us for lunch.

We went and that was when I found out about his dripping-wet walls and the gas space heater.

The lunch was simple, but tasty, and Kiki showed himself to be a decent cook. After we ate and the boys had their presents, we chatted. Kiki, it turned out, had a fascinating history.

When he was a young man, with no education, he had worked for a *grande dame* in the area, who owned a chateau some kilometres to the north. He had been a gardener and general handyman. Then Adolf got nasty and invaded.

Croutons and Cheese!

Kiki joined the *Maquis* and began to fight back, for the honour of France. Unfortunately, he had reckoned without the fact that the his employer was a Nazi sympathiser. Kiki's nocturnal activities – which basically comprised taking pot-shots at German soldiers and vandalising sections of railway – came to her attention and she promptly denounced him.

Fortunately the young Kiki was not at home when the soldiers came to get him. His family had managed to warn him while he was still at work; the *grande dame* did not wish for the arrest to be made on her policies.

So Kiki managed to escape the soldiers, but he had to flee into the woods. For the next three years, until the liberating forces arrived, he hid in them and lived on what he could find, along with food parcels that family and friends left in secret hiding places.

Living rough in the Burgundy woods in summer would be pleasant enough, and there would certainly be little chance of apprehension. Kiki explained that there were many like him, all fugitives. In due course they began to be supported by the Allies, with British bombers airdropping *matériel* and supplies at night. They became an effective insurgent force (yes dear, insurgents are only bad when they are on the other side) and for years, Kiki and his compatriots tied up German regiments that were much needed elsewhere.

The courage of these men and women is remarkable, but we should not forget the sacrifice that ordinary country folk made. The Germans knew full well that the *Maquis* relied on supplies from family and friends; not a few were rounded up and shot or sent to concentration camps. The German brutality only made the French more resolute; the sons of the soil are stoic if nothing else. But after the Liberation they vented their fury on those who had collaborated with the hated *Bosch*, including Kiki's erstwhile *grande dame*. He smiled as he told us how she had been taken to the main square in her home town and had all her hair chopped off. I think Kiki might have taken the head with it, had he had his way.

This was the standard punishment for a woman who had collaborated. Her locks shorn, her clothes would be ripped to expose her breasts and she would be paraded trough the streets, where people lined up on both sides hurled abuse and spat at her. The men, Kiki assured us, had it much worse.

I believe him. France was invaded by German forces three times between 1870 and 1940, which basically meant that three whole generations had known what it was like to live under a German jackboot. And on each occasion, the German forces had behaved atrociously, though, to be fair, their performance in World War II was a show-stopper. They treated the French with utter contempt and themselves as being above any kind of legal or moral constraint.

I was lucky enough to speak to a small number of people, Kiki being one, who had lived through Hitler's Occupation, and it opened my eyes. I learned then that there are some things you might possibly be able to forgive, but you can never, ever forget. Seeing the reactions of old men and women as they talked about that time – which ranged from tears flowing down their cheeks to shaking with anger and indignation, I came to know something of what they must have suffered.

And, they said, none of these invasions had been provoked. That is true. In 1871, in order to force German unification before a common enemy, Bismarck forged letters that led directly to the Franco-Prussian War. As a result of this, Germany annexed Alsace and Lorraine. In 1914 and 1940, Germay did not trouble with such niceties: it just invaded.

 I think it does enormous credit to French tolerance and forgiveness that they are prepared to be as friendly as they are towards the Germans. I am not sure I could be, if I had lived through that.

In 1944, Kiki participated in a major campaign to immobilise France's railway network in the run-up to D-Day. It was co-ordinated by British and Free French Special Forces who themselves ran dreadful risks. Unlike the Allies, The Germans relied almost entirely on the railways for the transport of troops, supplies and *materiel* over long distances. So compromising the system was an important war objective.

Later, Kiki's group made contact with the Free French forces under General de Gaulle that were making their way up from the south; he was with the Allies when they liberated Paris.

Kiki kept his rifle as a souvenir and went back to a simple life as a handyman for the rest of his days. On meeting him, there was nothing that would have suggested that this gentle and rather unprepossessing man was a military hero who had risked being summarily shot, had he been captured, for so long, or that he had done so many dark deeds. Of the hated Germans, he would only say; '*On les ai tué,*' and made a gesture as if firing his rifle.

Kiki was decorated, at the end of the war, for his unstinting sacrifice for France, and every year he was amongst the slowly dwindling number of veterans at the memorial on the festival days.

At the end of his life, Kiki became unable to manage alone and he was taken into a care home nearby. Perhaps it did not suit him, or perhaps someone who had been so free for so long could not abide being cooped up; in any case he died not long after.

Kiki was a very unassuming hero. He had faced extreme danger and hardship yet shrugged it off. He made nothing of it at all. He was not alone by any means.

In my life as a photographer and journalist I have been lucky enough to meet quite few like him, from all walks of civilian life. Photographers, actors, journalists, artists, artisans, academics and schoolteachers. Every one, I had to tease the stories out of. They did not wear their heroism on their sleeves. Yet they were indeed, heroes.

Kiki lived for France, and would have died for her. He never mentioned the privations he must have suffered, nor did he seek recognition for his acts. It had simply been his duty, he said, to fight the invaders.

The British Airmen

If you were paying attention in the last chapter you would remember that the *Maquis* were supplied by Royal Air Force airdrops. The planes used were single-engined Lysanders and a variety of twin-engined light bombers including the Bristol Blenheim. The latter, though groundbreaking at its introduction was, by 1943, obsolete in combat terms. However many remained in commission for tasks like this.

Their missions were flown at night, partly to avoid German fighters, but also to avoid giving away the positions of the *Maquis* groups they were supplying. They flew low, to avoid enemy radar. In World War Two electronic navigational technology was in its infancy and less than entirely reliable. This made flying low at night extremely dangerous, especially over territory that was blacked out.

One dark night in September 1942, a Blenheim set off on this dangerous mission. The aircraft carried a crew of three men, a pilot, a bombardier/navigator and a gunner/radio operator.

A few kilometres to the south of P'tit Moulin stands an isolated hill which was then, as it is now, thickly forested. At just after two in the morning the Blenheim struck the trees that covered the hill and crashed.

Instead of a catastrophic impact with the ground, the plane came to a progressive stop, slowed by the trees, which ripped off wings and engines but miraculously left the fuselage largely intact. Two of the men aboard, though injured, survived the crash while a third, the gunner, died of his injuries.

The sound of the impact was heard in the hamlet of LaVault, further down the slope. The alarm was raised; a group of men climbed the hill and discovered the wreckage. They pulled the victims free. While the men were still alive, they had been badly injured; one had a broken arm. They both had cuts and contusions and were shocked and concussed.

The rescuers put them in a horse-drawn cart and brought them to P'tit Moulin, to the *épicerie*, which, as it happens, is what my house used to be. The owners were known locally to be sympathetic to the Resistance. They fetched the local doctor, who patched the airmen up as well as he could. Then they were hidden in the barn loft(which readers may recall is full of straw to this day) and ordered to lie low.

Croutons and Cheese!

Fortunately the crash had not been noticed by the German occupying forces, so they were not yet out looking for the survivors. After passing a nerve-wracking day in the barn, the airmen were led to another refuge in the woods not far away. There they remained for a week, until the Germans were informed of the crash. They searched the site and realised that there were enemy aircrew on the loose in the area. The hunt was on and troops were moved in to apprehend them, while houses and barns were systematically searched.

The two surviving British airmen had sufficiently recovered to be moved and were taken, on a trip that lasted weeks, first into Vichy France, then south through the Massif Central to the Pyrenees, then across the Spanish border.

Although Spain was Fascist and Hitler had sent forces to fight for him, its leader General Franco had refused to enter the war on the Axis' side. Spain was neutral and combatants who entered would be returned to their country of origin.

Now all of this fascinating tale was completely unknown to me, of course. The first I knew of it was that the mayor arrived on my front door one Saturday morning waving a sheaf of white paper. At first I thought I might have contravened some obscure French law, but it transpired that I had not. (Actually I am sure I had contravened quite a few, but either the mayor did not know, or, far more likely, didn't give a hoot about it.) It turned out, after some thorny grappling with *patois*, that the papers were actually the text of a speech about what? An air crash?

To me, in my ignorance, this was quite the news. An air crash? In P'tit Moulin? When? And what did it have to do with me? The confusion was well up to normal standards.

After a little while it became clear, however, that the mayor wanted me to translate the text of his speech into English and then to read it out after he had delivered it in French. This would happen once at the church service, which was to begin at 3pm, and again at the *vin d'honneur* back in P'tit Moulin. Naturally I accepted, despite the fact that it was by then a little after ten in the morning.

We didn't have Internet then so I quickly called Antoine *le Potier*. Yes he had heard of it. He was planning to attend. A what? A translation? Okay. He proceeded, having divined my utter lack of comprehension, to give me the background to the story, pretty much as I have outlined it above.

Dealing with the mayor's speech was easy, since it was written in more or less standard French, so in good time I was ready. The service itself was held in the fine church at Épinac, eight kilometres away, where the unfortunate gunner was buried, and a healthy turn-out it attracted. After the sermon the mayor duly gave his speech and then I stepped up to the podium and read out the translated copy.

Later we rendezvoused at the *salle des fêtes* in P'tit Moulin, and for the first – and last – time I got to meet the heroes. The two survivors were still alive then, though it was fifty years after the crash. They were nice men from the north of England, both, by then, into their seventies.

The *salle des fêtes* had as usual been transformed with bunting, but this time there was an abundance of British and American flags. Before the low stage at one end, where ceremonies always took place, tables had been laid out. On them was a variety of historic warplane technology recovered from the site of the crash, including the radio set, sundry navigation instruments, a section of fuselage, a machine gun and, somewhat strangely, the tail wheel.

Once again the mayor delivered the homily and I stepped forward and read my translation again. It was well received and many who had previously regarded me as one might, perhaps, an unknown but presumably dangerous alien life form, smiled and later came to press my hand. I spoke at some length with the surviving airmen about this ongoing tradition and the outpouring of simple gratitude that the locals displayed; they were clearly deeply moved.

It was the mayor himself who explained what was going on. 'They risked their lives for France, monsieur,' he said, 'And one of them died for us. We will never forget them.'

Although the two survivors whom I met have both now passed, this statement is true. The site of the crash is overgrown and lost; the Moulinards may no longer toast the fallen and survivors in a *vin d'honneur*; but the artefacts recovered from the crash have been placed on show in the museum at Épinac, with an explanation of the story behind them.

Bûcheron Barbu

P'tit Moulin, as readers might by now have guessed, is not short of its characters. One such is Pierre Hublot.

Pierre is the village wild man. He possesses the unique attribute of not having appeared to age one year since I first met him in 1993. In all honesty I have no idea how old he is. I do know that he is a great-grandfather, which, at least, would suggest he was somewhat older than your esteemed correspondent. (That is my story; and I am sticking to it.)

Hublot actually appears to have been washed up on the high tide of 1968. He has never lived anywhere other than P'tit Moulin, save for his *Service Militaire* and a couple of other sojourns at the behest of the Great Republic; however we are told it was nothing too serious.

Pierre is not petite. He is a good six foot and has the body of a man who has worked hard in physical jobs all his days. However the general impression of scariness comes not so much from his height and breadth but from the fact that he wears his hair well past his shoulders and has a beard that reaches to mid-chest level. Somewhat reminiscent of the images we have of Viking berserkers raiding quiet Saxon towns. Or perhaps Gaulish warriors – but then, the Gauls shaved their beards. Vainglorious lot they were, and noted to be so by the Romans. But since the Romans hated the Gauls perhaps we shouldn't really take their word for it.

I digress (again). Pierre has, it would appear, been wearing the same set of clothes for the last twenty-odd years. Quite how he has managed this trick I have not yet been able to fathom, but I suspect perhaps he bought a job lot around 1970 and has just been working his way through them. Though if local rumour is to be believed, it was more likely a truckload of *vêtements* that got hijacked...

In any case, actually asking Pierre where he gets his clothes and how he manages this trick appears to be a little too risky even for me, and I have bearded (ho ho) some right scary people in my time.

To return to the beard, which is what has gained him his nickname, *Le Barbu*, this item is not too fussily maintained. This is a general condition of the good man's persona, but somehow the fact that his beard is perpetually yellow with tobacco stains, the consequence of his having a *caporal* permanently attached to his mouth, does tend to stick in the memory.

Actually that tobacco stain – and sundry remnants of comestibles – is the only sure way of knowing the exact location of *le Barbu's* mouth. This is because his moustache flows into his beard in one uninterrupted cascade of hairiness. It's not that I want to kiss him or anything, it's just nice to know things like that.

For all of the two decades that I have been associated with P'tit Moulin, Pierre has been one of the denizens of *Chez Angèle,* the cafe just across the road. That's the one with the alfresco *urinoir,* you recall. His taste for cheap red wine is prodigious to the point of being legendary and Pierre never lets a day go past without slaking his thirst at least twice. I am led to believe that he keeps bottles at his places of work too, in order to keep a steady state of inebriation at all times. One should aim for stability in life, after all.

Pierre is a *bûcheron,* which means that he is a full-time wood man. While one might have thought this *metier* might be falling out of fashion as a result of more modern forms of heating, this is not the case. Instead, the dwindling number of able-bodied sons of the soil prepared to do the hard work of the *affouage* – the annual thinning of the communal woods for firewood that was described in the first volume (hint hint) means that there is plenty of business for those who are still willing to do it.

Pierre is one of three *bûcherons* operating in the village. When you consider that there are under a hundred residents these days, this shows how popular the trade remains. They sell their logs either to locals too indigent to *affouage* themselves – like me – others with better excuses, to the people of the nearby towns who do not have the advantage of *affouages* themselves and, increasingly, to specialists who convert the wood into pellets for use in central heating boilers. This last looks to me like a lot of extra work *pour rien de tout* but it's all the rage these days. Damned expensive though.

Pierre *le Barbu* has several pieces of machinery which appear to have popped out of the same time-warp as he did. One is a terrifying self-propelled grab thingy for picking up tree-trunks, which are then suspended between chains in the after part while Pierre drives them back to his yard, up the hill from M. Rey's farm. You really don't want to get in the way of that thing. It has no cab, just a seat, steering wheel and the usual controls – well I think anyway, though I would not want to bet on the brakes. Just saying. Watching *le Barbu* careering about aboard this contraption – which would not be out of place on a *Mad Max* set,

Croutons and Cheese!

believe me – is quite the entertainment.

Pierre's other professional mode of transport is a tractor. Yes a tractor, but not just any tractor. This is a two-litre single-cylinder beast. To start it you have to use a decompressor – the motorcyclists amongst you might know what this is. And maybe the boat owners.

Basically it is a device which lifts the exhaust valve off its seat (pay attention at the back) and so prevents the engine building up compression inside the cylinder. So the starter, or the hand-crank in older days when men were men, can spin the motor up to a respectable number of revolutions per minute without groaning to a sad stop as the piston reaches the top of its stroke.

Once the engine is turning as fast as the starter, or the sweating human, can manage, you disengage the decompressor. This allows the engine to develop compression and the piston is forced through the stroke by the energy you have so vigorously built up in the flywheel, which on engines like this is humongous. (Though not as big as the one on the Gardner 4L2 I once possessed. Another time.)

With any luck, the operation, if timed precisely, will deliver joy and happiness as the motor bang-bang-bangs into life. If not timed so, it's back to the beginning in the hope that the battery still has enough juice in it to perform the trick again, otherwise you will be sweating on the end of that crank-handle.

Pierre's tractor is orange, and of rudimentary silencing, so its approach is fairly noticeable. If the colour and noise were not enough get your attention, the mushroom clouds of black smoke emitted would clinch it, I think.

Like the log-dragging monster, this has no cab and since he works for himself, no safety cage either. I get the impression that Pierre deems such precautions unmanly.

Le Barbu's other transport – his Sunday best if you will – is a beige Renault van. This is the same model as the farmers use, except older, tattier and – beige. Theirs, for some reason, are all white. You'd have to ask. In addition to the naturally unprepossessing colour scheme, time has added many a trace of darker brown as rust gnaws at the ancient bodywork.

This doesn't seem to exercise Pierre overly and as far as I can see the vehicle has no *Contrôle Technique.* Well, none of his do. I think Pierre feels that such concessions to Parisian bureaucrats and lawmakers are beneath a true *Gaulois*.

Pierre is intermittent in his communications with me. It appears to have something to do with the alcohol level. When he's really not very squiffy, he'll just sail right past, but when he's high as a kite and too drunk to walk, he'll actually pull over and attempt conversation.

This can be a little one-sided since my French tends to give out when confronted by someone with precious few teeth left, a *caporal* in his mouth, speaking in a ferocious Burgundian accent and using many words which, dear reader, do not feature in the Collins Robert – or any dictionary. And all this, mark you, when my interlocutor is so drunk he's having difficulty standing up.

I did wonder aloud to my friend Antoine *le Potier*, one day, why it was that Pierre never got done for drunk driving, not to mention the appalling state of his sundry vehicles.

'Oh, they used to,' replied my informant. 'They used to send out the new recruits to the Gendarmerie at Nolay to do it.'

'Really?' I rather thought, myself, it might be a job for an experienced hand. But Antoine, as usual, was ahead of me.

'Yes. If he doesn't ignore them, and they upset him, he shoves them through a hedge. That way the recruits learn...discretion.'

I nodded.

'He got jailed for it once. But he has eleven kids.'

'So?'

'You can't go jailing a man with eleven kids for a vehicle offence,' explained Antoine, carefully. 'The wife will give the mayor pure hell.' He shrugged. 'So now they just let him get on with it.'

'And insurance?'

Pierre sucked a tooth. 'My advice? Don't have an accident with him.' (Shrug.)

I was not really very reassured.

Despite the terrifying mien and reputation of the man, I, the humble mad Scotsman, have been able to get one up on Pierre three times.

The first was when I borrowed Antoine's own single-cylinder tractor to fetch my *affouage* – readers of the first volume will no doubt remember this. As I blasted up Grande Rue, the denizens of *Chez Angèle* trooped out to observe, and amongst them was Pierre. Neither scowl nor *caporal* moved, but I knew that despite himself, he was impressed.

The next time was on the occasion of the death of the late Queen Mother. I don't have a lot of time for royals, you know, being a republican, but still. The old girl seemed pleasant enough. News of her death came on Easter and it happened that *la famille* Fleming were all up the hill near to Pierre's yard rolling Easter eggs that morning.

Pierre hove into view in the chicken-shit coloured Renault and stopped some way away, squinting through *caporal* smoke and surveying the situation for possible risk. The mad ones were throwing eggs down the hill.

He drove up and demanded to know what was happening and I, as best I could, explained the tradition of painting eggs and rolling them.

'But you're not Christian,' he pointed out, and I had to agree.

'You're crazy then.'

I later discovered that Pierre wasn't referring to my religion, or lack of it. 'Not Christian' is pretty much a direct translation of 'uncivilised barbarian' or, in other words, Not A French Person. Anyway, at the time and ignorant of this nuance, agreement here seemed the better line. Then his eyes, normally bleared from wine and to be fair, thrashing around in open vehicles, brightened.

'*Anglais.*' It was a statement. It might also be his name for me. I'm not sure.

'Scottish.'

'Hmph (wave of hand). *Et la reigne mere?*'

'Dead,' I replied, in French, trying to sound concerned. I thrashed around for an idiom that summed it up. In English, I would have said 'But she had a pretty good kick of the ball,' but I knew no comparable French phrase so I just translated.

'*Mais elle a eu un bon jeu de foot,*' I said. Well I know it's a bit approximate but I was on the spot.

Pierre scowled and his eyebrows knitted together. I thought he might swallow the *caporal*. Then he roared out laughing, for the first time confirming the location of his mouth and also treating me to a view of his dentition – which was not a nice sight. Remarkably, the *caporal* remained steadfastly attached to his lower lip. He shook with paroxysms and, at last, gasped out *'SAUVAGE!'*

Still guffawing he shoved the Renault into gear and shot off up the hill, yelling, until he was out of earshot, *'Sauvage! Sauvage!'*

It was pretty funny you know. I consider that being called *'sauvage'* by someone believed, even by his fellow villagers, to be a Cro-Magnon throwback, something of a badge of honour.

The third time was when I was helping my next door neighbour with her drains. I'm nice that way. This is my part-time neighbour, an English woman who bought the house from the homosexual *ménage-a-trois* previously installed. (And you thought life in rural France was dull, didn't you?) Well, my neighbour, who shall remain anonymous, may not be quite so colourful but she can turn on the eccentricity when she has a mood to do so.

On this particular occasion she was clearing old shrubs from the border in front of her house wearing a short, sleeveless black cocktail dress, a pair of green wellies and gardening gloves.

'It's an old dress,' she explained, when my eyebrows betrayed me again. 'And it's too hot for trousers.' I could not but agree.

Anyway we were busily clearing when around the corner comes the familiar beige van, trailing its clouds of blue smoke. Whether this is burned oil from a worn-out motor or just the *caporal* is anyone's guess. Pierre – for it were he, of course – slammed on the anchors when he saw my neighbour and to my sheer astonishment suddenly came over all nice and polite. It was a rather gruesome sight.

Now my neighbour doesn't speak *le Francais* too well, and the Burgundian accent just kills her. And to boot she has a rich northern accent of her own, one which I have always found particularly attractive I have to say. In any case, Pierre *le Barbu* has no English. The result was that I found myself cast as interpreter.

Now Pierre is married, has eleven children, I know not how many grandchildren and even great-grandchildren. In addition, and if rumour were to be believed and in total defiance of logic, given the general crustiness of the beast, he has at least three mistresses. Despite all this and his (and her) fairly advanced years, it quickly became obvious that Pierre was chatting my neighbour up.

With politeness and bravado unexpected in the extreme, Pierre – while he neither removed the *caporal* nor got out of the car, became as winsome as a monster of his ilk could manage. He even smiled – well, I think that was what he was doing. The fact that he was as drunk as a lord did make it all a little tricky to work out, and understanding what he was saying was a real struggle.

Our hairy, bearded, drunken Lothario enquired after my neighbour's name, her health, her marital status, how long she might be planning to stay in P'tit Moulin and why she was wearing a cocktail dress at three o'clock in the afternoon – which last I have to admit made sense. I mean my neighbour is an attractive and sophisticated woman and she was carrying it off well, but it was, shall we say, a surprising garment to be seen worn about in P'tit Moulin, especially along with the wellies.

In the end, a huge lorry came around the corner and Pierre *le Barbu*, after having made it wait for a good five minutes, was obliged to move on, if only because by then the driver had his hand fixed on the horn and the noise was deafening. One can hardly verbally canoodle – especially through a thoroughly bemused interpreter – while shouting, and in the end, he was obliged to admit defeat; but before doing so, he gave me the most lascivious wink imaginable.

My neighbour and I then proceeded to nearly end ourselves laughing. 'All the same,' I cautioned her, 'I would lock your door.'

'Don't worry, I was planning to,' she agreed.

I am pleased to report, however, that she was not the recipient of a nocturnal visit from the amorous *Barbu*. Well, so she assures me anyway.

The Green Beans and the Giant Courgettes

During our first sojourn in France, Moira became an avid gardener. We had bought, as a part of our house, 1500 square metres of land. But it was not, as they say, contiguous with the building; oh no, this is France we're talking about and that would have been much too simple.

To be fair it is, by P'tit Moulin standards, just at hand, a mere hundred metres away. But to get to it we had to go out of the little door in the courtyard, across one neighbour's garden (she of the LBD and green wellies, these days) across another neighbour's land and finally to our own.

The land itself comprises a rather sweet little orchard, some ten by ten metres, and then a great long ten-metre wide strip of field. There's no water up there or electricity or anything, and no trees outside the orchard area. It enjoys – as they say – a sunny southern exposure, which means that in summer it is a parched desert where Beau Geste would have been thirsty.

Yet it was here that my lady wife decided to develop her talent as a gardener.

Not long after first coming to P'tit Moulin I came to realise a fundamental truth: there are always ten things to do before you can do whatever it is that you really want to do. And this of course, leads to a second observation: a lot of things you want to do never get done because you spend so much time doing the things that have to be done before you can do them.

From conversations with others I have discovered that this is a very commonplace phenomenon indeed. Everyone I know has a house full of half-finished jobs because there's a list of things they have to do first.

But back then we were young and naïve and did not think twice about how this might affect our lives.

Anyway, the water. The solution seemed obvious: buy a hundred or so metres of hosepipe and run it up to the field. Which we did. I actually still have the hose.

With the water supply organised the next thing to do was to cultivate the soil.

Now I have a confession to make. I have a pathological hatred of digging. I think this comes from a time, long before, when my mother had a house in Angus, where the soil was apparently 10% earth and 90%

stones. If I remember correctly from my long-distant schooldays, this is called 'boulder-clay'. Whatever, digging the damn stuff is a nightmare.

My darling wife had identified a patch some 15 metres by 10 metres where she wanted to establish her vegetable plot.

The soil in our field at P'tit Moulin field was really just the clay without the boulders. There's no way I am digging that, thought I, after a very brief moment – read milliseconds – of reflection.

There was no Internet in those days and one resolved issues like this through the small ads in the print media. I researched *Le Bien Public,* our local rag, which in those days was sold at the cafe and in a short while I found what I was looking for – a rotovator.

I had never used one of these but I remembered them from my childhood, when part of my parent's garden was used for produce. There was a fearsome orange machine with flying blades that Jim the gardener used to dig over the tatty patch with. And great job it did too. So I knew that was what I wanted.

Sure enough, a few days later, such a machine was advertised, offered for 1000 francs at a location near Dijon. Since at the time these beasts were around 5000 francs new, I wasted no time and hitched the old trailer up to my trusty Granada estate.

It was a filthy night of steady driving rain and finding the seller's place took a while, but eventually I got there. After the introductions I was led to the man's garage where he showed me the machine, a shiny blue and white beast.

'It won't start,' he said, apologetically. 'I only just tried it.'

I considered that it might have been more helpful if he'd tried it before placing the ad. That way I could have avoided a fifty-odd kilometre trip to get it, through pouring rain, when I might have been sitting tucked up warm in my house in front of the stove with a glass of wine.

'I think it's the coil,' he said, apologetically. 'I cleaned the spark plug.'

A quick pull or two of the starter cord confirmed it: no spark.

Otherwise, however, the machine was in very good condition and although old, had clearly been very little used. It was powered by a Briggs and Stratton four-stroke motor that didn't even seem to be leaking oil. I thought about it. A coil was not going to be too expensive.

We did a bit of that sucking of teeth and looking at shoes with our hands in our pockets – 'humming and hawing' in English. Don't ask me what the French is, but they do plenty of it.

In the end, he cracked first. 'Look,' he said, 'You can have it for 600 francs.'

That was sixty quid. I can never resist a bargain so I had it.

We lashed it onto the trailer under a tarp and I headed homewards, happy as a dog with two co...er, tails.

The next morning I manhandled the rotovator into my workshop and began to dismantle it. After taking off a few covers I was confronted with a huge flywheel, and I could see that the high tension cable to the spark plug exited from behind this. Logic (I'm good at that, really) said that the coil must be on the end of that cable.

It took a bit of ingenuity to get the flywheel off, but soon it was on the bench and there was the culprit – a standard induction coil, regulated by a pair of contact breaker points.

Well I had been for decades a motorcyclist and British metal at that, so I knew all about CB points – an instrument of hell invented by the Devil himself, in the form of Joe Lucas, Prince of Darkness. Not a vehicle in the world has had these curses for a quarter century and more now. Well, except maybe some Indian ones.

Anyway, I had a quick look at the points and sure enough they were black and encrusted. I cleaned them till they were shiny, with emery, reassembled the whole and tested for spark. Big, fat and blue.

Well that was okay, it only cost me an hour of tinkering and maybe a nail or two. I retired to the interior for lunch and a glass of wine in celebration.

Much – *much* – more challenging was actually operating the thing.

Now Jim the gardener's machine (you remember Jim don't you? Please keep up) had two big drive wheels with what looked like mini tractor tyres up front and the blades behind. It was sort of serious and functional. Operating it seemed simple enough, at least as far as I could tell from my childhood observations, always at a safe distance, you understand. You just pushed down on the handle bars that projected out the back to the depth you wanted, set the throttle and let rip. I'd seen Jim do it many times, it was easy.

This thing was totally different; the digging blades were at the *front*

Croutons and Cheese!

and the wheels were flimsy and not powered. How could this be?

Fortunately it had come with an owner's manual, which at first just confused the issue. The wheels, it said, were for transportation only and on NO ACCOUNT (in capitals) was the machine to be used with these in place.

Sure enough, they clipped on, held in place by a pin.

Hmmmm.

According to the manual – which fortunately was in both French and English – the idea was that you used the wheels to get the machine to the field, then removed them. This left the whirring blades at the front and a kind of spike at the back, upon which the wheels had been mounted, which was adjustable for height.

I understood that in order to make the thing dig, one was to apply no downward pressure to the handlebar, and when one wanted to cease and desist, then one pushed down firmly. This way the spike at the back would dig in and, at the same time, the blades would rise clear of the ground. Adjusting the height of the spike controlled the depth of cultivation. At the same time it acted as a brake, actually *making* the thing dig rather than just heading for the horizon at full blast. With me so far?

There was no accelerator on the rotovator, just a rudimentary choke and a switch with two positions, 'idle' and 'run'. At the 'idle' position, the manual said, the operator could leave the transport wheels in place and the machine would pull itself along using the blades. You controlled forwardness by a lever that tightened the belt between the motor and the shaft the blades were on. This was very much an off and on affair too, none of that gentle slipping of the clutch whatnot. Oh no.

I think, with the benefit of experience, that the writers of that manual were correct to insist that one should never leave the wheels on while the machine was in operation. I shudder to think of it tearing, unrestrained, across the countryside, devouring small animals and children. I wasn't really sure about it with the wheels off either, but never mind, I did it, and nobody died.

I manhandled this monster – it wasn't even a little bit light or easy to move – out through the courtyard, along the path over the neighbour's land, through our orchard and up to the field., the motor putt-putting away quite happily.

It was a fine day in mid-April, still cool although it was sunny. But I had broken out in a profuse sweat long before I got to the field.

I took a moment to catch my breath and summon my courage,

then I turned to. This was going to be an entertaining moment, I could just tell.

The Briggs & Stratton was actually a side-valve motor, a design that must have originated in the 1920s. Still it seemed harmless enough; why, pottering up the path it had almost seemed tame.

Things were about to change.

I removed the wheels, just as the manual told me to, still thoroughly perplexed as to how this contraption actually worked. I pushed the throttle down to the 'run' position, where it was held by a detent. Immediately, the machine's cheerful 'putt-putt' changed to a baleful, ear-shattering roar that made it seem a great deal less benign. No *Thomas the Tank Engine* smiley face now, this thing had horns.

I was already pointed in the right direction, so, full of trepidation I pulled back the clutch lever and off we went. And I do mean 'off'.

Have you ever seen those videos on YouTube where some old biddy is out walking her daughter's (I hope) Newfie when it spies a cat and all you see is flying horizontal elderly lady?

It was a bit like that. Except I am six foot and 90kg. So horizontal is tricky for me. But I got close, with legs windmilling to keep up. I had to wrestle with the totally-counter intuitive idea that the less I pulled back, the slower it would go and the deeper it would dig. If I pulled back it went faster, in other words. It's not easy to master that when you're concentrating on keeping a powerful machine from heading across your neighbour's patch and off to Épinac. Or somewhere.

Once I got something like the hang of it going in a straight line, I had to learn how to turn corners. This was even more insane and reminded me of driving a motorcycle and sidecar – an equally implausible mechanical contraption that requires massive amounts of force on the handlebars to control it.

But, although I did gather a crowd of onlooking well-wishers – or maybe they were just worried about the potential havoc I might wreak – I did actually get the patch rotovated. When I finished I was in agony, every muscle screaming, running with sweat and panting. It felt like I'd been wrestling with this mechanical fiend for all of two hours, but on checking my watch, I discovered that in fact I had done the 150 square metres in under half an hour.

Well impressed I was.

As ever, Antoine *le Potier* was my conduit to what the local buzz was.

'I hear you got a rotovator,' he advanced, the next time he passed.

'Yes,' I said. 'I did the vegetable plot with it.'

'I know,' he replied, thoughtfully. 'I heard all about it. Is that the way you do it in Scotland? Because nobody here ever saw one used like that before. They were impressed.'

Quite exactly what the locally-approved method was he never actually happened to appraise me of. Judging from later observation of others operating similar machines I was not alone in being somewhat confused.

With experience I found out that the trick – funnily enough, as the manual had said – was to get the height of the spike right. This depended on a lot of factors but mainly how hard or wet the soil was. It was very much trial and error, but once I had figured out how to get the rotovator set up right, I found I could just click the clutch lever into its detent and the machine would work itself, quite happily digging to the required depth with a minimum of control or effort.

Like so many things, once I'd finished the job, I knew how to do it.

Now I have a confession to make. I am the world's worst gardener. I don't know why. I apparently have a magenta thumb (photographer joke; magenta is the complementary of green.) So I think it was fortunate that my dear wife actually planted the green beans that the plot was mainly intended to grow. That way they had a decent chance of survival, whereas if I had planted them they'd never have poked their bonny little heads through the surface of the soil.

They were dwarf haricots, which grow independently and don't need to be held up on a trellis. (I know, I read the packet.) All we had to do was water them.

The other delights set out by Moira were courgettes. These too seemed to be doing very nicely, I thought, as I watered them every evening. We left the hose in place through the week, only rolling it up at weekends; it would never have got done otherwise and that field can be parched in summer.

Unfortunately, as the beans came to ripen, Moira had another of the bizarre and terrifying turns that so marred our sojourn. One morning she fainted and after getting her to bed I called the doctor. He was sanguine. 'It's only to be expected,' he said, reassuringly. (Not.) 'This is how it goes with multiple sclerosis. But she's had some time in remission, so let's not panic.'

Well, that was what I think he said. My French still wasn't that hot then.

Moira was confined to bed. She complained of extreme dizziness and a terrible sharp tingling sensation all over – to which the doctor just nodded, gravely. *'Sclérose en plaques,'* he would mutter again and again.

However, this time nobody suggested steroids or any other drastic solution; just bed rest, painkillers and tranquillity.

Of course she couldn't walk, so this presented a problem with the darn beans.

I don't know if you know anything about beans, so I'll assume you don't. In P'tit Moulin, at least, a haricot is able to grow from around two centimetres in length to eight in 24 hours, more or less. Sounds great, huh? The trouble is, two centimetres was too short for my beloved, and eight was too long. She likes *haricots extra fines* which are five centimetres long.

Thus I found myself baking under the arid sun twice every day, trying to catch the little sods before they got too big.

I did wonder whether the increased consumption of beer required by this did not rather cancel out any saving from growing one's own beans, but this was not a subject for discussion.

The other plants we grew up there that year, the attentive among you may have noted, were courgettes. Now I imagine there must be a 'courge' for there to be a diminutive of it. But no-one ever discusses that. In Blighty they're called marrows, but there are no 'marrowettes'. Go figure.

Anyway, courgettes have the same propensity as haricots. They'll splurge from a diminutive 15 centimetres long – not really big enough – to 45 overnight. Remarkable.

We were not the only ones to fall foul of this super-growth on the part of our beloved vegetables. Everyone in the village knew that Moira was ill and they were all very sweet and helpful. I got used to opening the front door to find packages of rather large *haricots verts* and colossal *courges* left on the doorstep. It was very kind.

We also grew tomatoes that year, in the courtyard, where they actually did very well – and suffered from the same profligacy. But all was not lost; a survey of my trusty Good Housekeeping showed how to bottle all of these and I soon had vast pans of ratatouille simmering

Croutons and Cheese!

away on whichever beast we were then using – I think it must have been in the first one. We had over forty one-kilogramme *bocaux* (Kilner jars) to keep us through the winter. So I guess it was all right.

As to Moira, after two weeks of agony, she just got up one day and said, as she had before, 'It's gone.'

It had, and it never came back. But we lived in its shadow – whatever it was – for years.

A Tale of Two Cheeses

There used to be a lovely cheese man who came to the market at Épinac. He was big and fat – I think it's the product testing – and he came from somewhere in the Jura with a seemingly endless supply of the best Jurassian cheeses.

The Jura is a region in the east of France, in the foothills and lower slopes of the Alps. The land is of limited value for arable farming, except in the lowest parts of the valleys, so dairy farming has been the mainstay for centuries, perhaps even thousands of years.

For those Anglophones whose conception of French cheeses begins at Camembert and ends at Brie, with maybe a detour past that garlic-flavoured spread stuff called Boursin (actually okay on sandwiches) then there is a surfeit of riches in Jurassian cheese that you can never have dreamed of.

De Gaulle complained, 'How can you govern a country that makes 264 types of cheese?' It's a fair point you know, and last time I checked there were actually over 600. That is a lot of different cheeses.

Our man at Épinac routinely had about thirty, which is a fair selection, all from small artisanal cheese makers in his area. At that time I could easily get enough cheese to last a week for 50 francs, five GBP. It was funny how, on the last three days, the little lumps of cheese got meticulously divided in half, so that on the Tuesday there was nought but a taste. But it was enough, washed down with rough red from the local *cave*. Lunch was always a long affair in those days and a fair bit of reflection was done on the comestibles.

You know I don't like to burst the French bubble, well, not too often, but they were not in fact the world's first cheese makers. The earliest we know of were the Greeks, who made a cheese from goat milk that was probably not dissimilar to modern feta. Around 1184 BCE, Homer mentioned a cheese called *Cynthos*. Later, Aristotle (384 to 322 BCE), commented on cheese made from the milk of mares and asses.

One of the most important agents in modern cheese-making is rennet. This comes from the stomachs of calves and contains an enzyme that curdles the milk. Previously this was done by bacterial action, similar to the way yoghourt is made. Rennet is more predictable and produces better results. This technology was known by 127 BCE.

The Romans, who adopted Greek culture wholesale, became industrial cheese makers and exported the product throughout the Empire. It was they who brought the expertise and technology to France. Well, it was Gaul then but you know what I mean.

Having said that, the French did do rather well at it, leading to the aforementioned 600 cheeses. They also invented the technique of maturing the cheese to improve its flavour.

There are so many wonderful cheeses from the Jura that it would be impossible to list them all, but I might just mention a few now that we are here.

Did you know that the same producers often make two completely different cheeses depending on the time of year?

Vacherin or Mont d'Or is a soft cows' milk cheese with a washed rind that was once known as a poor cousin to Comté. The cheese is extremely soft and spreadable, particularly at the end of the ripening process, which is why it is traditionally presented wrapped in an a spruce wood belt to hold its shape. It is normally served cold, spread on bread, but can also be heated. Mont D'Or is only made in the winter, while the same producers make Comté – the king of hard cheeses – in summer. This is because it only takes 7 litres of milk to make a kilo of Mont d'Or against 12 for a kilo of Comté, and in the winter, when the slopes are covered in snow and the cows are inside being fed on hay, this is a more efficient use of the available milk.

Cheeses encircled in wood, like Mont d'Or, have been made since the 13th century. Although there is no doubt that cheese was being made in the Alps before then, monks from various abbeys pioneered dairy farming and cheese making as we know it today. They cleared forest to create high pastures for grazing in the summer to produce rich milk and practised transhumance, where the cattle would be herded up into the mountains for the warm summer months and then returned to the abbey to winter indoors. Remember *Heidi*? That stuff.

An excellent variation on Mont d'Or, which our lovely cheese man introduced me to, is *Écorce de Sapin*, literally, 'pine bark'. Here the cheeses are matured on planks of oak and the wrapping, instead of being a sliver of wood, is actually a strip of pine bark, This gives the cheese a very distinctive flavour (would you be surprised to learn that it is a bit 'piney'?) which is wonderful but can repeat a bit. So if you're prone to that sort of thing, perhaps best avoid.

Comté is the most highly-prized hard cheese made in the Jura, and perhaps all of France. 45,000 tonnes of the smelly stuff (of which more later) are produced each year, more than any other French AOC cheese. Comté cheeses are famously huge. A round is 65 centimetres in diameter, weighs up to 40 kg and contains 450 litres of milk. This cheese keeps very well, which was an important consideration in the past, in order to get through the long winters. By making their milk into cheese, communities could preserve dairy products. In addition, dry, hard cheeses were easy to transport and sell. It's best in the late summer and autumn months, when it has had six to nine months or more to mature.

Beaufort is produced exclusively above 800 metres, with cows' milk from the *Tarine* breed, this cheese is named after the Beaufort valley where its production began in the Middle Ages. Today, it is also produced in Maurienne and Tarentaise. After production nearly ended in the 1950s, *Beaufort* was saved thanks to the establishment of producers' cooperatives. It remains a cooperative product, made from the milk of several herds. An essential ingredient in Savoyard *fondue*, *Beaufort* goes well with mushrooms, particularly chanterelles.

Raclette is the best known cheese of the French mountain resorts, although it was originally made in Switzerland, in the Canton du Valais. It is normally melted and eaten with potatoes, *charcuterie* and pickles.

A fashionable delight of *fin de siècle* French table culture was the 'Raclette' party. We still have them although I daresay they might be seen as terribly *démodé* by the chatteratti in Paris these days. The way it works is you have a sort of grill/hotplate thing that you put in the middle of the table. You can fry meat and vegetables on the top or just keep stuff warm. Everyone gets a little metal pan that goes under this. So you cook whatever you fancy having on the hotplate, put it in the little pan and then cover it with a slice of *Raclette*. Then you slip the lot under the grill and allow the cheese to melt over everything.

Hours of fun.

Reblochon's name comes from the Savoyard word 're-blocher', which, in the 16th century, meant 'second milking', slang for cheating or fraud. Beginning in the Renaissance, tenant farmers paid their rent in cheese, the amount calculated on the volume of milk their cows yielded. Landowners or their deputies verified this, but in order to reduce the quantity of cheese demanded, the wily farmers did not milk their cows completely till after nightfall when the inspector had left, whereupon they completed the milking and kept the cheese made from it for themselves.

There are numerous excellent hard or semi hard cheeses called *tomme*. Usually they are in rounds of one or two kilos and have a characteristic charcoal-grey rind which smells lightly of ammonia. They were originally considered 'peasants' cheeses', and not of the same standard as the grand cheeses like Comté.

Tomme de Bauges has been produced since the 17th century. The milk used in its production comes from *Abondance, Tarine or Montbéliarde* cows. A variant is Tomme de Savoie, also excellent. These cheeses are very fruity in flavour but still delicate. My personal favourite is Tomme de Chèvre, which is very similar but made from goat milk. Whereas the cow-milk tommes are buttery in colour, Tomme de Chèvre, made from goat-milk, is pure white and slightly translucent. Excellent nibble.

First made in 1975, Morbier is a fruity, semi hard cheese from the village of the same name a few kilometres from Morez in the Haut-Jura. It is made in flat rounds of around five kilos. Made – as are all the best cheeses – from unpasteurised milk, Morbier has an unusual feature, a thin layer of charcoal in the middle. When it is cut this shows as a black line. It is rather delicate and goes well with white or rosé wines.

So, what can you do with all these cheeses? Well you can eat them. Usually, cheese is served after a main course and before – please note, Anglophones, *before* – the dessert. It's supposed to clear the palette or something. You don't eat huge lumps of bread with it, although you may finish up the hunk you just used a part of to clean your plate. (This is dining with friends, you understand; we do not do this in five-star restos.)

This is because, in social dining, you'll probably not get a fresh plate for the cheese; so unless you like your Mont d'Or all covered in *bouef bourguignon,* then best wipe, *n'est-ce pas?*

Generally the cheese board will be passed around and you help yourself to two or three small morsels. If the particular piece you fancy is getting small, then it is polite to take only half. (This may lead to infinitely-reducing cheese. But never mind.)

It is very common to open a nice – perhaps the nicest – bottle of wine with the cheese. In the days when I maintained a cellar, I was never short of invites on the strength of the bottle I brought *'pour le fromage'.* But in the end I drank that.

It was entertaining.

You can cook with cheese too. Everyone knows about pizzas and *pommes au gratin,* but there are a few things you can do with Mont d'Or that are just amazing. One is to heat the entire cheese in the oven and then plonk it on the plate alongside carrots *juliennes,* celery, biscuits, etc; you just shovel the cheese out with these. Burp.

Another very satisfying dish is to parboil potatoes and sauté some onions and garlic. Chop or slice the potatoes and mix them with the onions, then lay the mix into a shallow bowl. Invert enough Mont d'Or cheeses (You can also use *Raclette)* to cover and place in the oven. Wait 30 or so minutes and serve. That's it – one of the simplest meals ever. And wonderful.

Comté is one of the most versatile cheeses. When cooked it doesn't separate, unlike cheddar and makes a brilliant cheesiness to the sauce that will string very nicely. Or you can grate it into soup along with some croutons...just the business for a cold winter day. Croutons and Cheese!

When we moved back to Scotland, third son on the way, we continued to spend as much time at our dream house in France as we could. Usually I would take a month in the summer and maybe a couple of weeks in spring and autumn. It's a long drive from Scotland to Burgundy, but it was worth it, especially when the children were young.

Croutons and Cheese!

At the time we lived in a house with a big basement and I, of course, had a wizard wheeze. Since I was already shipping as much wine home as the springs on my Rover V8 (known locally as the *Dukes of Hazzard* car, on account of its straight-through race exhaust) would let me, why not diversify and bring back some cheese? I know I could just have popped down to Edinburgh and stocked up from the wonderful Valvona & Crolla in Elm Row, but while they have the best Italian cheeses outside Italy, they were not quite Jurassian, you know? So why not bring a couple of hundred pounds' worth of cheese back?

Soft cheeses freeze very well, so that would not be a problem. Hard cheeses don't, they separate and sweat, but there was that grand cellar... and, coincidence of coincidences, there was a long disused meat safe in the back garden. For those who don't know, a meat safe is a wooden cupboard, but the sides are made of perforated metal sheet, so the air can circulate but the flies can't get in. Or the mice.

With some difficulty I got this into the cellar. It was always a bit tricky down there because there was only 5'6" headroom, but I managed it.

So with all in Scotland prepared for the Great Cheese Delivery, off I hied with the boys to France. Moira didn't come that time, I can't remember why. Maybe she had a premonition.

At the last market day in Épinac before we were due to return, I made our cheese man very happy indeed. Huge chunks of Comté, a whole *Raclette*, lots of Mont d'Or, *Écorce de Sapin*, Morbier...what a surfeit of richness.

I can't remember if there was a *Tunnel sous la Manche* then, but in any case we were headed for the ferry. It's a long thirsty schlep up the autoroute from Beaune, but we did it in six hours. Although the day was overcast and cool, we were aware of a certain....odour, and kept the windows open a crack.

I remember all went well as we boarded the ferry at Dover; as usual we locked the car and went up to the lounge decks. The boys always liked to be outside and so did I, and in those days, ferries actually had places you could do this.

The car decks on those ferries are often pretty warm, and as we returned to the car I was aware of people around me wrinkling their noses. The reason became obvious when I opened the car door.

We piled in, I opened all the windows full and turned the fan on full blast. I wouldn't say my eyes were quite watering, but it was a close thing.

We were more than happy to get out of the close confines of the ferry and onto the motorway. We had arranged to stop overnight at Moira's parents' house in Woldingham, south of London, and there we made our way, arriving in the gathering gloom of evening. Shattered, we fell into bed.

In the morning, John, my father in law, passed the breakfast table. 'Peculiar smell out there this morning,' he mused. I just concentrated on my coffee and croissant, while reading the *Times*. (That John read this woeful Tory rag always amazed me. Or maybe he just got it when I was due to visit.)

The drive from Woldingham to Arbroath was, let's be honest, smelly. Actually it was more than smelly. It was nauseatingly so, and this despite the fact that the cheese was very well wrapped.

'Pooh,' said Moira as she helped unload the car. 'What is that *smell?*'

'The cheese,' I replied.

'Really? how much is there?'

'Dunno – couple of hundred quids' worth.'

'Oh,' she replied, feebly.

Well, the soft cheeses were quickly frozen and that put an end to their assault on our nostrils. But there was still a third of a Comté, cut into chunks, alongside some others that could not be frozen. This was where my Cunning Plan came into effect-- they would be stored in the basement, in the old meat-safe that I had installed there. You remember.

I don't know if you know this, but French houses have solid masonry floors over their cellars. In older ones, these might be supported on stone vaults. So there is quite a bit between you and the cheeses you store down there.

Not so in Scotland. The floors in our house were tongue-and-groove Baltic pine. And being over a hundred years old, the boards had eased a bit and so they provided less than a perfectly hermetic seal.

As the autumn wore on towards winter, I think we grew inured, even though the smell percolated all the way to the top floor of the house. Meantime we were eating so much damn cheese I though I might turn into one.

But if we became inured, others did not. When my mother came round – you remember, the one I lost – her face would have that perpetual look of 'there is something smelling really awful in here but I am too polite to actually mention it', and when we did explain – as we had to, every time she visited – she would just smile pleasantly, nod and continue to grimace. My aunt stopped visiting altogether, claiming it was too hard on my uncle's system.

My neighbour buttonholed me one day to ask if I had smelled it, and wondered if we should report to the council that there was a problem with the drain. 'Nothing dead in your cellar, is there?' he asked, all sweetness and light. When I explained that it was the cheese and I would give him some, he paled, shook his head and looked at me as if I were mad. 'I hope you'll do something soon,' he appealed. 'My wife has angina.' (This exchange, by the way, somewhat dramatised, made its way into another of my excellent books, called *Poaching the River*.)

We managed to finish it at the New Year Party. I think we felt we had done our duty by cheese. I was never tempted to repeat the exercise, and went back to buying from Valvona & Crolla.

That way they got to live with the stink.

A Bull in the Back Passage

Now one of my neighbours, of the horny-handed persuasion (well what else, here?) a certain Henri Carnot, once determined to buy himself a bull.

Henri was fed up paying 'service' fees to other farmers, you see. To explain this, imagine that your farm is actually a harem filled with nice sexy big white Charolais cows. Well, then, they need a bull, obviously. How can you make little Charlies without one?

So what you do, as the owner of a *troupeau* of said nice white Charlie cows who has no bull, is hire somebody else's to do the business. You wait till your cow is in an amorous mood – technically called 'bulling' – and then you take her to see Big Charlie and you watch from a distance to make sure all goes well. (I don't advise this for the weak of constitution; the act of coition in bovines is, erm, spectacular, and have you seen the size of a bull's balls? You get the picture.)

The problem is that your chum is not going to let his bull have some love for nothing. I mean he is a farmer, we may safely presume, since dentists rarely keep prize Charolais bulls in their back gardens; mark you, this is France. Anyway, assuming that Charlie's owner is indeed a son of the soil then he wants paying for his bull's *amour*, and this is called a 'service fee'. The euphemism for coition being 'to serve'.

Our Henri decided he would circumvent this process, save some money and buy himself a bull. Henri is, to put none too fine a point on it, cheap. So he was going to have to find a cheap bull – no easy task.

Now, I can see you just twitching to tweet me about why didn't Henri just raise one of the male calves his cows must have delivered and save a small fortune? Well that is *most* astute of you, Pernickety of Godalming, but it misses the point. Bulls have to be pedigree. That means, come with the stamps and verified paperwork. And you will need this if you intend to sell their offspring as genuine Charolais beef. They are fussy about that in France. So not just *any* bull will do: it has to be the proper sort of bull. Are you keeping up all right? Good.

Our horny-handed hero applied himself to the task, though, while the rest of us whispered to each other amusedly that he would probably end up with a bull with three legs.

Henri may be cheap but he's not daft. He knows a bull needs all four legs to mount a willing and winsome cow. So he wasn't going to waste his money on a bull with three legs, for goodness' sakes.

Instead, he got a bull with one eye.

No, I am not making this up. Some farmers can be a bit remiss about dehorning their cattle. When I was a lad (oooaaarrr) and worked on a farm myself (you didn't know? Oh well) we used to 'disbud' the horns. We did it when the calves were only a day or two old, with a thing like a big electric soldering iron. Made a hellish smell. Then they never grow in. The horns I mean. But some farmers do it the old way and cut off the pointed end of the horn with a saw later. They say, and I hear their argument, that cattle use their horns for scratching and it seems a shame to deprive the poor dears. Or something.

However, in order for the horn to be cut off it has to grow in the first place. (Logic.) And young cattle, particularly male beasts, like to rough-house. A lot. Bit like rugby players only even less bright. (Maybe.) So they quite often stab each other accidentally. (Which is why we used to disbud them at three days. But I digress.)

Cattle being pretty tough and having extremely thick skin, this usually is no more than a scratch or two, but it seems our Charlie (Henri's putative purchase, do keep up) had a more serious altercation with another bull. It was probably over politics or religion, football not being of great interest to bovines on account of having four legs. In the resulting pissing contest 'plop' went Charlie's left eye on the end of his opponent's horn. The one on his head, I mean.

Now the thing is, most farmers are a wee bit superstitious and a bull with one eye, you know...It's bad luck. It must be. Or something. So poor Charlie had no buyer and it looked like a one-way trip to the knacker's yard for him. Cow pie. Well, bull pie.

But not our Henri. He was a great one for the *fraternité* and *egalité* stuff. He was no man to judge a bull by the number of eyes it had. And anyway, he reasoned, the part he was interested in was at the other end, so as long as that worked and the price was right, well then.

He reckoned that provided young Charlie could identify the rear end of a cow and didn't try to shag any white Renault 4 vans in a case of mistaken identification, it was all good. Henri would give Charlie a new lease of life as official progenitor of baby charlies on his farm, and at a knockdown price too; I mean he hardly paid more than the cost of the meat, it had to be a deal. Or so Henri thought. What was that our great Bard said? Oh yes... 'The best laid plans of mice and men gang aft agley.'

But doubts of this deep and philosophic nature were far from Henri's mind, snuggled under the flat cap that appeared to be glued on to his pate. (I've actually seen it. It's pure white and smooth as a baby's bottom. His pate, not his mind.) Having agreed the price, the only question that remained was. 'Could the one-eyed bull actually do it?'

Now a wee aside. You do get gay bulls.

No, I am not kidding. Homosexuality has been identified in over 1500 species of mammal and *Bos taurus* is one of them. So Henri, being a wise son of the soil, required to see Charlie do the biz before parting with the hard-earned. I mean if he had been a bit of a limp-fetlocker it would not have been any good at all at all, now would it?

So a long-lashed beauty in an interested condition was selected from Henri's herd and trailered over to *chez* Charlie. And our two horny-handed hayseeds, Henri and Charlie's owner, leaned on the fence sucking on stalks of grass (at a safe distance) to observe while Charlie demonstrated that there was nowt wrong with *his* stalk and he was as red-blooded a straight bull as there is, all the way through, yessirree bob and not only that but he knew the difference between a cute heifer and a Renault 4, in case you were wondering; all with associated bellows, shouts, moos, heaving breath, rolling eyes and, inevitably, the entire vicinity being, erm, splattered. I mean seriously if it was bovines that made porn instead of people...OMG. As my daughter says.

Anyway the suitability of One-eyed Charlie (as he became known *chez nous*) for the job opportunity in question having been established beyond any doubt, cold hard cash changed hands and he accompanied his by now doe-eyed *amour* back to Henri's in the trailer.

Well, Charlie settled in to his new role very nicely. He was a sweet sort of a bull, rather good natured. Charolais are like that. As a point of information, the beef breeds are usually fairly docile, although you can never fully trust a bull. Generally it's the dairy bulls you have to watch. Mean sods and deadly with it. But if in doubt, stay out.

Anyway old Charlie liked to have his ears scratched and the usual things cattle enjoy, such as a little bit of fresh hay or grass. But as with all bovines he was a curious beast and had a sense of adventure.

Now in cattle, 'adventure' doesn't mean skydiving or anything like that (thankfully; though there is something charmingly surreal about the idea) but it does mean getting oneself out of whichever field one is locked in and going for a mooch around the policies. And to this end they will worry, annoy and pester fences, gates, bolts and locks until they open. I mean cattle aren't that stupid; they see Farmer Jack (or in this case *Fermier* Henri) sliding that bolt every time *he* closes the gate. How much nouse do you think it takes to wonder if playing with the bolt a while will open it?

Well however much that is, Charlies (and all other cattle forbye) have it. So in no time at all young Chas was getting a reputation for himself as an escapologist.

(The alert reader will have noted that this is a popular pastime amongst the non-human residents of P'tit Moulin.)

Now a word about topography. P'tit Moulin is built into the side of a hill. That means that the ground behind my house, for example, as roughly three metres higher than that in front. For me this isn't too much of an issue because here the slope is relatively gentle. However, two doors further along where my neighbour Jacki lives, it's a different story.

The ground immediately behind his house is three metres higher than the ground upon which his house is built. Now that would cause a case of damp like you would not believe, so somebody, presumably the long-interred builder of said house, had excavated along the back of it and built a masonry retaining wall. So there is a sheer drop of three metres into a trench that runs the whole length of Jacki's house, and it ain't a small one.

The existence of this trench was not obvious, because our thoughtful first builder had returned his retaining wall so that it came back to the corner of Jacki's house. This was to prevent the ingress of the nefarious ones intent on breaking into the house and robbing the owners.

But the effect – since there are no windows in Jacki's house at ground level to the rear – was to create a masonry enclosure roughly 20 metres long (told you it was a big house) by one metre wide at the bottom. It's a bit wider at the top because for good structural reasons the retaining wall leans a bit.

I wonder if you can imagine what this might mean, in practical terns? Yes? Well, it was a trap with walls three metres high on all sides, with no way out. So Jacki thoughtfully left a ladder propped against the end wall, on the inside, so that, you know, if one fell in and did not actually break one's neck, one might escape. Jacki's good that way.

Along the top of the retaining wall was a thick hedge, about a metre from the edge. So there was a path between the hedge and the pit.

At both ends were gates, always bolted. This arrangement was in place to stop any idiot taking a short cut home from *Chez Angèle* falling into said man-trap. You can't say they didn't take precautions.

But what works for humans – even a mortally pissed son of the soil – does not necessarily work for bulls.

You see, the trap runs roughly east to west. The retaining wall is to the north and the house to the south. At the eastern end there was a fairly non-committal sort of wooden gate between the trap and the hedge, more a deterrent than anything else. But at the other end there was a much more masculine affair altogether, a solid steel gate with a padlock, set on steel posts well knocked in. This was because that gate could be seen from the road, and it was more serious so it would put off any passing *cambrioleurs*.

It happened one fine day that our four-legged hero, Charlie the One-Eyed Bull, got out of the field he was in, which, as it happens, was just up Grande Rue. He must have wandered down the hill and then turned into the lane at the back of my house, then past my neighbour – she of the cocktail dress. Then he discovered the little wooden gate and must have thought that was interesting, since there was no other way out of the garden except the way he had come and you know, it's no fun to do that.

So he just pushed over the wooden gate. A Charolais bull can weigh three-quarters of a tonne and Charlie wasn't petite. Then he ambled his carefree way along the narrow passage between the hedge and Jacki's retaining wall. Bear in mind that in doing this he was proceeding in a westerly direction, which meant his right eye was to the north. You still with me?

The problem was that to the south, Charlie had no eye at all. When he got to the serious big hairy-chested gate at the far end, he realised – doubtless after a bit of shoving and worrying – that no, this one wasn't going to be a pushover, and he would have to go back the way he came.

But the passage is only a metre wide and Charlie was getting on that width. Bulls aren't famous at going in reverse, so he probably decided, 'Hang it, I'll have to turn round.'

At which point, because he had not seen the trap to his left, he having no eye on that side, he found himself in free-fall.

Well Chas was a lucky sort of a lad. The ground at the bottom of the trap had never been concreted and so was just soft earth, and he managed not to get himself all out of line on the way down. But now he was in a pen with walls three metres high that was only just wide enough to fit in. Kinda like a crush, you know? You never worked on a farm? You missed out.

Well, Charlie, having doubtless given the end wall a couple of good dunts, realised that he wasn't going to get out that way, and so he decided to call the cavalry.

The first I knew was when the kids came in and started jumping up and down. 'Dad! *Dad!* There's a bull in Monsieur Ferrault's hole!'

It took me a second there to assimilate that, but when I did I followed – well was dragged – out the back gate of our courtyard where, sure enough, I could hear the most heartbreaking roaring. Following this I discovered Charlie's trail of destruction, and then the bull himself, looking decidedly confused, pawing the ground, bellowing and generally acting Not Very Happy At All – and surrounded by three-metre high walls.

Well it was actually quite funny you know. So I sent Calum to find Henri, while the rest of us went round to Jacki's front door.

Jacki hadn't a clue, because he's a bit deaf and there are no windows in the ground floor at the back, maybe a good thing. But he followed us round so he could get a look into the trap. Charlie was mollified now, since the kids had been throwing him handfuls of hay.

'Tsk tsk,' said Jacki and sucked a tooth. I know what he was thinking. 'How much is *this* going to cost?'

So it were perhaps as well that just at that moment, Calum returned, followed by a somewhat out of breath Henri.

After the customary shaking of hands, he too, had a peek over the edge. I think he was wondering the same thing as Jacki. Well, it was Henri; he rarely thinks about anything else.

I took a look again. 'You're going to have to knock out that end wall,' I pointed out. 'Either that or you crane him over the house.' I made a kind of crane gesture with my arm and the kids sniggered.

Sometimes the Frogs don't know when I'm joking, you know. Jacki and Henri both waved their arms around in horror. It's pointless to say 'I was just kidding.' I'm an honorary *Anglais*; I therefore do not *have* a sense of humour. Henri was certainly thinking of the money and Jacki was probably thinking what might happen if three quarters of a tonne of Charlie were to slip off the hook and land on his roof. It doesn't bear thinking about.

'We'll take the wall down,' said Jacki, firmly. I nodded.

'But the ground is a metre higher on the outside than it is down there,' I pointed out. 'You'll need to put in steps or something.' I could hear Henri groan as I said this, but Jacki nodded. He was beginning to get the idea.

'Yes.'

After some protest – because Henri did not want to pay a builder for steps – our good son of the soil agreed that he would take down the wall himself and Angèle's son-in-law, who *is* actually a builder, could use the stone to build some steps. This seemed a reasonable compromise, so off Henri went to fetch some tools as well as a bale of hay and some water for Charlie.

So it was, after a long day, which involved putting up a temporary barrier to stop Charlie trying to get out before the steps were finished – or maybe the builder just didn't fancy being on hands and knees with a one-eyed bull behind him, who knows what ideas he might have got – and with the westering sun dipping on the horizon, One-eyed Charlie was led to freedom on the end of a rope.

He's a right docile beast that one, I have to say. But I think in the end, he turned out less of a bargain than Henri had hoped.

Jacki, on the other hand, was well and truly delighted. He had the access to his back wall he'd been wanting for years, with a nice new set of steps and it didn't cost him a penny.

Man-Trap!

Ever seen a real man-trap? I don't mean a hot blonde in heels either.

My neighbour was given this with a load of other bits and bobs. She thought it was a toy, but closer examination made me disagree. For a start, it was quite clearly a gun of some order, but it didn't have any kind of handle. There wasn't a conventional trigger either.

It might have been a toy cannon, but it didn't have a carriage. Opening it up revealed that it was chambered to take a real twelve-bore

shotgun cartridge. Plus it's made of very heavy cast iron. It's just not like a child's toy at all.

We scratched our heads over another glass of wine while I played with it. Then I saw that the hammer, when cocked, was held back by a simple hasp. This had a lever on the end with a hole in it. That was when the penny dropped.

'It's a trap,' I said, trying not to sound like that Dagon look-alike in *Star Wars*. Three French faces swivelled towards me – my neighbour, her son and another local, a *vigneron*.

'A trap?' quoth they, somewhat disbelieving.

'Yes,' I insisted. 'This hole is to attach a trip line.' I cocked the little weapon, and with the lightest of pressure on the lever, the hammer snapped down. 'Like that.'

Immediate disbelief was followed by a rush to the computer, where my neighbour's son set to Googling.

And this is what we found. The little gun is indeed a trap – a *'piege de braconnier'* in fact, which means 'poacher's trap', though maybe a better translation would be 'trap for a poacher' judging by this advert, from 1967. It turns out you mount it on some suitably sturdy piece of wood, lead the trip line to your door, or across a path that an intruder might use, and then BANG! Lights out; a very effective 'man-trap'.

Well, the advert we found does specify that this was only to be used for blanks, but another site noted that 'while these are not illegal, after numerous accidents involving such devices loaded with live cartridges containing shot, their use was strictly controlled.'

Live cartridges? Accidents? Bloody hell, I'll say. That thing could blow a sizable hole in you. It is distinctly lethal. Even loaded with blanks, you'd probably drop dead of a heart attack.

Anyway, they're apparently not that rare (which says something) though I had never seen anything like it before. So I thought I'd share. Meanwhile my neighbour is cleaning it up to put on display. I did offer her a couple of cartridges to try it out, but she declined. Very wise.

Cops in France

Les Flics: just as you can't write about life in France without discussing wine, you can't write about it without discussing that greatest of scourges, the bugbear and bane of everyone's lives and a daily topic of conversation all over France, third only to the weather and politics. And what are *les flics*? The cops, of course.

Mostly, when the French talk about *les flics,* they are talking specifically about traffic cops, who are universally regarded with almost unlimited contempt and no respect at all. However, when the occasion merits, they expand the concept to include any other kind of cop who's been getting in the way of the French being French.

Antoine *le Potier,* for example, just the other day was bemoaning the fact that he had been fined by *les flics* because he had been doing 65 kph just inside the Beaune town limits.

'It's an outrage! I was already slowing down,' he said. 'You know that the limit is 50 kph in all the towns? Well, now they insist that you are doing no more than that when you pass the town sign. It's ridiculous!'

Like anyone else living in France, I had long been aware that the French regard the town sign, or the first speed-limit board, as the point at which they begin to decelerate, and the rate of deceleration depends on how much of a hurry they are in. At the same time, the first sight of the town exit sign is the point at which to begin accelerating, not the passing of the sign itself.

These two facts together mean that they can go through small villages without ever getting below 65 kph, yet will stoically insist that they strictly observed the speed limit throughout.

Antoine also had a little incident with the gendarmes from Bligny not long ago. Now before I begin this tale, I feel I should put to rest a belief that has become, according to my children, current in the UK in the last few years.

This is that the gendarmes in France are not real police. Well, they are, and this is a classic bit of Anglo-Saxon, er, confusion. I believe it has even been aired on Stephen Fry's television show; not that that would make it any more the truth.

So let me explain.

Firstly, the gendarmes are indeed police, as understood by any Anglo-Saxon. The term literally means 'men at arms' and they are descended from the peacekeeping forces that first appeared in the Middle Ages, when local lords and later, town councils, would hire the biggest, toughest bruisers they could find; and set them to breaking the heads of troublemakers and then throwing them in the stocks.

Today, they retain full powers of arrest, of handing out fines, impounding vehicles, hauling you up before the beaks and shooting you. I suggest you exercise caution before expressing any quaint notion that they might not be 'real' policemen. They have a long and proud history, tend to resent having it belittled, and a posh accent cuts no mustard here. Just saying.

I think the situation is complicated for Anglo-Saxons, well, the English anyway, because although the gendarmes are indeed The Law, there are other forms of police as well, notably the police. British people are not used to this, though the septic tanks might be.

The organisational difference between the gendarmes and the police is this: The gendarmes are police who have full civilian jurisdiction but whose responsibility is to the Ministry of Defence. This does not mean they are military police in the way that a Brit or a USican would understand it. They are real police and they can and will nab you and worse. The police are police just like the gendarmes, but they answer to the Ministry of the Interior. It is worth noting that these days you need a Master's degree or equivalent to join the police, so don't try to be clever with them.

Simply put, the gendarmes are military police with civilian jurisdiction and the police are civilian police with civilian jurisdiction. Clear now? The gendarmes have blue cars and the police have jam sandwiches.

They both have the same powers but here's a thing to remember: the police – who are all armed – can only fire on a suspect if he or she attacks them with deadly force. The gendarmes can shoot you if you resist arrest or try to escape. So of the two, I'd be inclined to be more wary of the latter.

So let us list French police in order of…how does one express *mechancité* in English? Meanness, perhaps. Well, the least virulent are the *Police Municipale*. To a Brit, these are a bit like Traffic Wardens on steroids. They often drive around towns on *Mobylettes* or in little vans, and don't normally carry heavy ordnance. They can still hand out tickets and on-the-spot fines, though, and otherwise thoroughly ruin your day, if they want to.

Then there are the aforementioned gendarmes, who are your common-or-garden, one-size-fits-all, regular Plod. They wear blue uniforms and carry automatic pistols. Their cars are blue and have the word 'Gendarmes' on the side. Every town has its *gendarmerie*, and that is where you go to file complaints, do any police-style stuff, and appear when you have been naughty. They are the primary enforcers of the law and investigators of crime. And they are as intolerant of transgressors as plod anywhere. Treat them with respect.

In major cities, there are indeed police who call themselves Police. These are the aforementioned civilian police, the *Police Nationale.*

Possibly, if you never strayed outside central Paris, you would never see a gendarme. Outside of major cities, in the smaller towns and the countryside of France, the Constabulary are called gendarmes and that is that. Says so right here in my trusty *Collins Robert.*

Similarly, if you live your life of Gallic hedonism in the countryside, you will probably never see a member of the *Police Nationale.*

On the roads, you will often see what look very much like police, with blue vehicles like the gendarmes, but with *Douanes* written on the side. These are actually Customs. They hang around the parking areas at the ferry terminals, and at the 'aires' or service stations on the motorways. They seem to really like machine-guns and very big dogs.

France is a Schengen country, which means that it has open borders; no customs controls, unlike in England, where there is always some officious little shit with the title 'Customs' asking questions he (or she) has no business knowing the answer to, well, not in a free country anyway.

The *douaniers* are not out to arrest, beat the holy crap out of you or otherwise ruin your day, they just want your money, and the way to get them to take it is to not have the appropriate papers for whatever it is that you might have in your vehicle, also with you. Brits, of course, are brought up to leave their documents at home, as a security measure.

The opposite is true in France. You are expected to carry all and any relevant documents, all the time. The sensible thing to do is to keep your receipts for everything you ever buy, your insurance, MoT, driving licence, dog licence, whatever, in a nice big bundle and stuff all of it in the glove box of your car.

That way there is a good chance you might actually have the receipt showing that the gallons of wine causing your car to ride on its bump-stops were bought legally, and if you don't, a slightly less good chance that the *douanier* will give up halfway through the pile of confetti and wave you along.

By the way, the oft-quoted 'limit' of ninety litres for the amount of wine that a UK citizen can buy in France and bring home to guzzle, is a complete red herring. It is only a 'guide' thought up by those shits, sorry, nice people at the UK Customs. It is not in any way enforceable in law, and you can bring back as much cheap (or otherwise) glug as you like. Same applies to cigarettes, if you have the evil habit. They have to actually prove that you intend to sell the stuff once you get back…and you wouldn't do a thing like that, would you?

They must find it amusing, in the UK Customs, that the English have done the ultimate cut-off-the-nose-to-spite-the-face and voted to put an end to privileges said Customs have been trying to take away for decades. This, apparently, because they dislike the Poles; yet without Polish pilots and their staggering bravery in the Battle of Britain, England would now be a part of Germany. So much for gratitude. For the French it just confirms what they have always known: *les Anglais* are insane.

Anyway, to get back to Antoine and the gendarmes. He told me one day that he'd just been stopped at the crossroads at Pont d'Ouche – a notorious plod hideout – for doing 120kph in a 90 zone. The gendarme, as usual in these cases all stiff and haughty like, explained to him that he had been driving 30kph over the speed limit, and that the punishment for this was 80 Euros and a point off his licence. Antoine, after a moment's thought, politely countered that his speedo had been saying 90, and he had not gone past this. The gendarme, sniffily, looked inside the car and shook his head.

'Your speedo is *stuck* at 90,' he pointed out. 'No wonder you didn't know you were over the limit. That's another 40 Euros for the defective speedometer.'

Now this is where the logical mind of the Frenchman can be seen to best advantage.

'Ah,' says our potter, 'I see. But if I didn't know I was speeding, I couldn't have known I was going over the limit, as you say, sir. So how can you charge me for breaking it?'

At this the gendarme, apparently, frowned, sucked a tooth, and went to discuss matters with his colleague. After a few minutes he returned, his mien grave. 'All right,' quoth he, 'You can either have the speeding fine or the defective speedo. Which is it to be?'

Antoine thought about this for about 0.5 seconds, and then made sure he had the details correct.

'It's 80 Euros and a point off the licence for the speeding, yes?'

The gendarme agreed.

'And 40 and no endorsement for the speedo?' Once again, the officer affirmed.

'Umm, okay, well, I'll take the speedo, thanks,' said Antoine, absolutely convinced there must be a catch. But there wasn't. The nice gendarme (who wasn't such a bad lad after all, it seemed,) duly wrote out the faulty speedo ticket and relieved Antoine of 40 Euros, in cash.

'Get it fixed,' he said to Antoine, before saluting and waving him off.

I swallowed my beer slowly as I percolated this. 'That's amazing,' I said. 'In the UK they'd have hit you for the speedo, the speeding, and taken your car apart to find out whatever else they could fine you for as well.' I shook my head and cast my eye over his ageing SAAB, which was parked across the road. I could see a half-dozen vehicle faults without even standing up.

'Oh, *bah non*,' said Antoine. 'That would not have been reasonable.' He shrugged.

'But you've fixed the speedo?'

'No. Why? I already paid the fine.' Antoine shrugged again and swigged his beer. 'I'll do it for the next *Contrôle Technique*.' He chuckled. 'It was a damn good job he let me off with the speeding though. I only had forty with me and it's a long walk back from there. Plus they'd have impounded the damn car and I'd have had to pay to get it out again.'

Fortune favours the bold, even in France, it seems.

Antoine's Pyrotechnical Delight

Antoine *le Potier* is a fascinating character. He was always up to some new scheme. The funny thing was that even the most hare-brained of these had a basis in logic. I think it's the French education system myself.

Take, for example, his famous wood-fired kiln.

Antoine, as should be obvious, is a potter, and a very good one at that. He is also a fine academic who researches his projects thoroughly.

Although he has many interests, at the time of which we speak, he was fascinated by the world of the Gauls, those ancient ancestors of the French people. Burgundy happens to be particularly full of Gaulish monuments and historical sites alongside the Roman ones.

Antoine very much liked the form of Gaulish pottery and worked hard not to reproduce it, but to create a style of his own that celebrated it. He was successful. He researched and replicated ancient Gaulish glazing techniques too.

Somewhere along the line he became interested in the fact that the Gauls – not having gas or electricity – fired their kilns using wood.

This tantalising tit-bit sparked a fury of research – and all in the days, mark you, before the Internet.

Book after book was sourced from the library as Antoine hatched a scheme: he would build himself a wood-fired kiln.

Now that might not sound too onerous a task, but you don't know Antoine like I do. See, he's French. So where I would probably have done the research and built a copy of a Gaulish kiln, he had to improve on it.

Air-flow, temperature control. all of these things – they became the stuff of post-prandial conversation. Construction methods, design, capacity, you name it.

You may not know this, but the Gauls had industrialised ceramics production early in the first millennium, They were a pretty smart bunch. The Roman historian Pliny the Younger noted, on a trip through Gaul, the variety and complexity of the agricultural implements they used, including a form of combine harvester pushed (yes, pushed) by oxen.

The Gauls, before the imposition of Christianity by the Romans, were Goddess-worshippers. All over France, thousands of ceramic reproductions have been found. These mostly show a triple-goddess, the centre of the Gaulish pantheon. And as I mentioned, they left countless other bits of pottery.

These were not produced in small domestic kilns but in large industrial ones. The Gauls had a factory system long before Henry Ford came along. These figurines were being produced in their tens of thousands, just like those of the Virgin Mary that one can find today.

It was this that Antoine, naturally, aspired to, and even to improve upon.

Now, as I may have mentioned, Antoine is French. Being French has consequences. One is that you are meant to respect the hierarchy. If the senior men tell you something, you're supposed to tuggy-forelock and agree. Antoine...is not really like that.

Once it got out that Antoine was planning to build a wood-fired kiln, he began getting visits from the other potters in the area. I know, I was there when many of them appeared.

Every single one told him he was wasting his time. That a wood-fired kiln could not be made to work. That he should concentrate making pots and stop that nonsense. That there was nothing wrong with a gas kiln, it was also a reducing kiln and far more efficient – in addition to which, Antoine already had one.

(For those unfamiliar with the weird and wonderful world of pottery, kilns come in two forms. Some are oxidising; these are electric and leave the oxygen in the air inside the kiln. This causes the chemical glazes to oxidise at high temperature. The other form is 'reducing' which is all we had before electricity. These burn fuel and so consume the oxygen inside the kiln. As a result the glaze reduces. These chemical reactions cause different colours from the same glaze.)

Unanimously, the other potters decried the idea of a wood-fired kiln idea as foolish and impractical. You could just see Antoine thinking, 'I'll bloody well show you.' In French.

He wasn't having any of it. The more people told him he couldn't do it, the more determined he became and as well as that, the bigger the project.

'I want to be able to throw 80-centimetre diameter pots and fire them,' he said, one day. Not many people could actually throw a pot that big; this was bravado, surely?

His true moment of inspiration came when he discovered Japanese wood-fired kilns. This was the vindication he needed. If the Japanese could make them, then a Frenchman could too.

Soon drawings were appearing on scraps of paper, left lying on the kitchen table. Genius was at work.

Naturally I became a willing accomplice. Our man had identified a nearby commercial pottery that had closed. In it, he said, were two huge gas kilns. Potteries, it turned out, usually have several kilns to that production is not interrupted during the actual firings.

'I need the refractory bricks out of them,' said he.

'Is that legal?'

Antoine shrugged. 'The roof has fallen in and the building will surely be demolished. The bricks will just go for landfill. At least I'll be recycling them.'

Which I thought was fair enough. Our Antoine's explanation was good enough for me, and I already knew that the way to explain anything you can't, or don't want to explain in France is to pretend not to understand a word of French. This technique had served me well in the past and I was prepared to rely on it again – though as it happened, I didn't have to.

We actually had to demolish one of the kilns – which was large enough to walk into. Over a couple of weeks of evenings, we removed enough of the refractory bricks to fill the bill. When I say 'bricks', though, these weren't your average firebricks. These were blocks some 10 inches (25 cm) on each side, and they weighed as much as you might expect. We required much beer after our trips.

Many of the blocks were not cubes but slightly trapezoid, because they had formed the vaulting of the kiln roof.

'Those are the really important ones,' said Antoine. 'My kiln will have three vaults.'

Antoine is a bit like me; he thinks in three dimensions. While he does make drawings (so do I), the global concept is retained in a three-dimensional model that only exists between his ears. The drawings are just to sort out the fiddly details. So nobody else involved – me and the ubiquitous cousins – really knew what we were building, as the project advanced.

When it was complete we stood back in awe. The kiln was three metres square and consisted of three chambers. The first was about 120 centimetres high and 60 cm wide, the second about 170 high and 80 wide and the last a full 2 metres high and 90 wide. They were all 2.5 metres deep. Their floors were built so that each was 50 cm higher than the one before.

The first chamber, Antoine explained, was the firebox. Flames from this passed through a row of flues into the second chamber, ran up to the ceiling, through another set of flues into the final chamber and then out into a chimney, again through a series of floor-level flues. So the hot gases passed all over the walls and vaults of the two firing chambers.

These dimensions, of course are only those of the internal spaces; the walls and roof were massively built of refractory brick inside and standard brick cladded. The whole was supported by massive steelwork, and over the lot was a corrugated iron roof.

We were all pretty impressed when it was done, and Antoine said 'We have to leave it for six months now, to dry out.'

'That'll give you time to make the pots, I remarked, cheekily.

The sourcing of materials and the construction of the kiln was done in May and June, and by mid-November, Antoine proclaimed the kiln ready to test. (And he had made enough pots to fill it.)

Before the first official firing, he had three test firings to make sure the kiln would actually work and it would not explode. The first showed that the cold kiln didn't draw properly, so Antoine fitted an electric fan to the top of the chimney to provide forced ventilation. It was removable so it didn't get cremated once the kiln really got going.

That fixed, along with a few details of the doors, Antoine pronounced he was satisfied. The first official firing would be the following weekend.

Outside the kiln was a covered space large enough to hold sufficient wood for a firing. Antoine reckoned that ten *stères* should be enough to do it. A *stère* is a metric cord – that is to say a metre cube of firewood, including the air-spaces. So that is a lot of wood. My house, when it is full and running a complete wood-fired central heating system, uses about twenty *stères* for a whole winter. Half that was going to go up the kiln chimney in three days flat.

Before anyone mentions it, I will here point out that burning wood as a fuel is sustainable, which gas is not. The forest that supplies the firewood is regrown once it is cut. So the system is carbon-negative. Carbon dioxide released into the atmosphere by burning timber is absorbed by the new trees growing. Using wood as a fuel is a good idea, as long as you can deal with the smoke.

Croutons and Cheese!

The firing, Antoine estimated, would take around three days. During this time the firebox would have to be constantly replenished with wood, so a squad of helpers and to be enlisted. I stood to.

The firing itself was spectacular. Antoine started on Saturday morning and by lunchtime the kiln was well alight and drawing properly without the fan, which he removed. As the afternoon wore on, I took over from him to let him rest and at nine, one of his cousins took over from me. A chain of firemen was ready to see the thing through.

Ceramists use things called 'telltales' which are little cones of ceramic material. These melt at different temperatures. They are placed inside the kiln where they can be seen through a tiny aperture, itself blocked, when not in use, to prevent cold air entering. Usually three are used, each melting at a higher temperature than the previous one.

By mid-morning the next day, the first tell-tale in the first chamber had collapsed. By early evening, the second in that chamber and the first in the larger, were obviously melting. We began to smile at leach other, we the loyal firemen and the others who had come to see.

But as the temperature goes up, so it take longer to increase it. By the end of the second day there was still no sign of the third telltales melting. Indeed the second, though they were obviously going, had not really collapsed. That meant the kiln was stable at around 1000 degrees. Antoine needed another 250, and the stock of wood was beginning to look too small.

Perturbed, he brought in another four *stères* of timber, good dry oak. All through that night he worked, like a wild-eyed demon tending the demonic furnace of hell itself, his face glowing red in the firelight.

I thought about it. 'Maybe you need to restrict the flow of air. Slow it down. Keep the heat in.'

(It happens that I have a Degree in sculpture from the days when one actually learned how to make things, so I know about this stuff.)

Antoine's face went from obviously worried to, 'Why didn't I think of that?'

He climbed the scaffold around the chimney and placed a tile over the flue, reducing its size to about an eighth.

Within half an hour the second telltales had collapsed and things were looking hopeful.

By lunchtime on the third day, tired and thoroughly blackened, our skin taught with heat from the flames, we rejoiced as the third telltale collapsed in the larger chamber. The whole oven and everything in it, was now at 1250 degrees. It was definitely time for a beer.

Of course, it takes days for a big kiln to cool enough to open it. Just allowing cold air in can shatter the pots. What you have to do is block up all the airways and let the kiln slowly cool down.

On the following Saturday, Antoine called. 'I opened the kiln yesterday. It's all OK. Come over.'

We all hopped in the loyal Ford Granddad and off we went. Sure enough, Antoine had the doors off the kiln and was slowly emptying. The day was raw November and cold but the kiln was still so warm I had to take my jacket off near it. Antoine was gently ferrying pots out, using heavy protective gloves.

'They're still about 400 degrees,' he said. 'But that's OK, they're fine. I won't be able to get the big ones till tomorrow, though, it's too hot in there.'

We toasted the kiln in good Burgundy wine and stayed for lunch. All the firing crew were there and we had pizzas – cooked in Antoine's own *four a pain*.

We each got a beautiful pot for our help; I still have mine.

Antoine always held an *exposition* just before Christmas, and that year it was furnished with the contents of the wood-fired kiln, including some huge and beautiful planters. Antoine invited all the other potters in the area. I think he did it just to see their faces.

Lizards and Lezardes (A Riddle)

I am fond of one but less so of the other; the one runs round the walls of my courtyard, and the other runs round the walls of muy house. The one is quick as lightning and the other, thankfully, is static. The one I do my very best to encourage and the other I would dearly like to be without. Have you guessed it yet?

Well it's a trick riddle. *Lézards* are the pretty little green and brown reptiles that scuttle around the courtyard in summer and which I am very fond of. I like to watch them and apparently, they like to watch me. Well, at least they observe me, staying stock still and watching me with one unblinking eye. Which is all very cute and dandy when we are talking about a 5-inch long *Podarcis muralis*, but I bet it would be a lot more sinister with a full-size *Deinonychus* – you know, the ones that made all that mess in the kitchen in Jurassic Park. Except the film-makers confused them with *Velociraptor*. Since *Velociraptor* was about the size of a modern turkey and *Deinonychus* stood twelve feet tall and had teeth and claws to match, I don't think I'll be getting Speilberg to guide me around any Jurassic wildlife attractions.

Anyway, my little friends are a threat only to various small forms of insect. They are better known as the Common Wall Lizard, and that's where they live – in the walls. So it's nice if you don't do your pointing too thoroughly, or alternatively build a couple of pretty dry-stone walls, to give them a place to live. They're very cute on hot days when they come out in the sun to warm up, and stand only on two feet at a time, one fore and one rear, giving the other two a chance to cool. Don't ever be tempted to try to catch one; all you'll have is a tail in your hand and a lizard with a stump.

We had one such once, which had been mauled by that pesky aviating mog, Speed Christmas Sherry, he who had been trodden on and jumped onto the stove hotplate – not on the same day. He was lodging with us as his adopted humans had gone on holiday…it's the least you can do. Anyway he brought this poor mangled thing in and it was quickly rescued by one of the boys.

It must have been mid-September by then and the lizards only came out on warm days when there was plenty of sunshine.

So now we had a lizard, still alive but only just, *sans* tail, and several children all totally distraught and beseeching us to call the vet.

Well, I had had enough of vet fees by then so I put the foot down and insisted that we would do nothing of the sort and instead, do what we could at home. I could just see the vet's face.

It happened that we had a tiny plastic aquarium that had once housed a goldfish – by then long since passed – that, I reckoned, would make a grand vivarium. So the kids gathered some moss and stone to make our new house-guest comfortable and then we placed her in the vivarium, which we hung up near the stove, where we thought it would be decently warm, you know. Meanwhile I did some investigating, being pretty clueless about lizards.

It transpired, the Goddess of the Internet informed me, that lizards needed live food. Well the only live food I could think of was flies. In those days there used to be a lot of flies in summer and autumn, but there are far fewer now. I don't know why, because there seem to be just as many cattle. Anyway, this proved to be champion fun for children, who were already deadly with the plastic fly-swats that were our first line of defence against the horrible beasties. They swapped their swats for those fishing nets on canes and set to catch live flies and putting them in jars. They were pretty good at it too and soon our lizard was being well fed indeed.

But it didn't seem to work. As the days shortened she became more and more lethargic and appeared for less and less time, until one day, she vanished altogether.

And that was that. I put the vivarium complete with everything in it, on the shelf in the pantry it had previously occupied, amidst much sadness from the progeny, and life went on.

Now it turns out that occasionally, being the kind of messy sod that wouldn't clean out the vivarium before storing it, is actually a good thing. As the days lengthened again, with our house-guest long forgotten, the place began to warm up. One day, Moira was fossicking about in the pantry looking for I know not what, when she shrieked.

'Probably a spider,' thought I. But I don't let my family members kill the eight-legged, I just show up with my jam-jar and piece of card, scoop them in and out to the courtyard. (To let you in on a trade secret, this doesn't work; the spider always comes back to her home. But if you don't tell the women-folks that, they'll be appeased for the time being, which is all that matters.)

So I fetched the jam-jar and the card and headed for the pantry. Moira was staring, eyes narrowed, at the vivarium.

'Something moved in there,' she said, in a voice that suggested she had just seen one of *Deinonychus*' beady eyes staring at her through a hole in the wall – or the time-space continuum as it would have had to have been. Since I was pretty sure there wasn't a five-dimensional wormhole in the pantry, I was not alarmed but fetched a torch and had a good look. And sure enough, there was a beady eye looking back at me, but it was only about two millimetres across.

'Well what about that? The lizard's alive.'

'Really?'

'Yes, let's get it out in the sun. It's cold in here.'

So we did and pretty soon were rewarded with the sight of our lodger, all spick and span and complete with new tail – you could see the join but never mind – crawling around the vivarium. It turned out that she'd only been hibernating.

When the kids came home from school for lunch, we organised a ceremonial release into the wild for her. I hope she did well and had many babies. And didn't eat them.

The other 'lizards' are in fact *'lézardes'* (what a difference gender makes, hey?) which are the cracks that run up the wall on the front of my house. They have been there since we bought the house, and I have a picture from 1890 (not 1990) that shows they were there then; yet everyone in the village seems to think they are getting bigger. (I know they're not because I measured them. Not moved in 23 years.)

You'll see a lot of old houses with cracks like this in the walls in France and you shouldn't hit the panic button. In almost all cases it is because the roof-trees – the *charpente* – which has been there for hundreds of years – has begun to sag.

As your roof is a triangle with sides of fixed length, if the apex comes down, the base must get longer and this pushes your walls out the way.

The old roof-trees were held together with big wooden dowels or 'trenails' but these shear under the onslaught of time and weight. Remember that a roof of old small tiles weighs a hundred kilogrammes per square metre just in the tiles alone, and a fair old bit in the timber, so a one hundred square metre roof – which is not that big – weighs over ten tonnes. If you have cracks, check these trenails. If they are broken and the tenons they are meant to locate have slipped out of their mortises, it's time to get in an expert to inspect your timbers.

Often you'll see massive tie-bars inserted at upper-floor level to combat the *lézardes*, but it's not the right solution. What you need to do is to strengthen the roof-trees, adding new cross-pieces and tying them in well, so that the base of the triangle cannot spread any more.

This will actually work, whereas tie-bars, which will be more expensive – and who wants iron bars flying through their house-- will not, and just cause horizontal cracks to add to the vertical ones you already have.

I am delighted to report that the reason my *lézardes* are not getting any bigger is because some thoughtful soul in the past has installed just such a system, nicely triangulating the roof together. And the *lézards* in my courtyard are getting along famously, thank you.

Dinner Parties and Escaped Cows

Dinner parties in P'tit Moulin can be interesting. A little while ago I was invited to a friend's house, with a number of other guests. Le repas, as ever, was wonderful, a *blanquette de veau* (it does not do to be squeamish at French dinner parties) done to perfection by the hostess. We had finished the main course and were mopping our plates with our lumps of bread in preparation for the cheese; at informal French meals '*en famille*' one is not normally given a fresh plate for this. It saves on the washing-up.

I was busy uncorking a rather nice *Nuits St Georges* to go with said cheese when I noticed that our hostess, who was sitting opposite me facing the window, was staring out of it, laughing.

'What's wrong?' I asked.

'There's a cow outside,' she said.

I looked round and sure enough, there was a large white Charolais grazing happily on her lawn.

'Oh, I'll deal with that,' I said, setting aside the *Nuits*, not without some sadness. But life's pleasures are sweeter when one has to wait. Or so they say. As I approach the end of my sixth decade I become less sympathetic to this view. But never mind.

It happens that I have some history in agriculture, having once worked as a Dairy Herd Manager. I even have my certificate from Bicton College of Agriculture. Aaaaar boy. But perhaps that can wait for another tome filled with witticism.

Out the happy – and replete – legion sallied to chat about her state of independence with Jacinthe (Bluebell in French). As we approached I took the lead. The animal was too far away to me completely certain of its sex, especially in the gathering crepuscule, so I casually mentioned to the others, 'It might be a bull, so be a little careful.'

With widened eyes they lost no time in hanging back and letting me take the lead. Well, I am the experienced one and also an honorary *Anglais* – so dispensable. Hmff.

Anyway, Jacinthe was indeed Jacinthe and not Jacques, so having established this (you can tell by the udders, it's a dead giveaway) I asked her what she was doing and suggested that she might be happier tucked back up in her field for the night.

She gave me one of those 'Do I have to?' looks, like a child being told it's past eight, time for bed.

I was firm. 'Yes.'

'Oh, okay,' she sighed, turned around and made her way out of the gate and up the hill. Now of course I had no idea which field she came from, but she did, and in she went happy as Larry. Or Lucille.

Which illustrates the power of gentle persuasion. If I'd made a fuss and a holler (as my dinner companions might well have) she'd have taken off up the road to Jours en Vaux and vanished, leaving us with some explaining to do to her owner, who would doubtless not have been best pleased to go cow-hunting at nine pm when the blessed beast would have gone home anyway, had we just left her. (This once happened to me with a herd of over a hundred Friesians. Another day.)

Anyway I followed her to her gate and closed it behind her. The bolt had no chain on it, always a bad move. Cows may look thick but they're curious and they'll annoy a bolt like that till they get it open... and then off they go.

Jacinthe (as I now affectionately knew her) came up to the gate as I bolted it. I rubbed her poll and ears while telling her in no uncertain terms to leave the bolt alone and I that would be advising her owner to put a chain on it the next time I saw him.

'Moo,' she said.

'Goodnight,' I replied, and headed back for the *Nuits* and cheese.

When I first began coming to France I was a bit surprised by that French habit. Not the one of having cows in the garden, the one of not changing plates between main course and cheese. These days I do it myself, but I remember my surprise the first time I sat down for a meal like this. I was twenty years old and a friend of mine and I had decided to visit another friend who was Breton.

We knew his surname and the nearest village but that was it – St Morieux in central Brittany. By dint of adventure that we have not time here to relate, we actually found the village and went to the local cafe, where we asked. Astonishingly, nobody had a clue who we meant, and the fact that our French was miserable didn't help. It turned out, apparently, that our friend had the same surname as over half the population in a 20 kilometre radius, so we were a bit scuppered.

Then I blurted out, 'He was in Scotland.' Our friend, Daniel, studied English at university and had been a language assistant in our home town the year before.

'Oh *that* one!' exclaimed half the patrons of the bar we were in. 'Why didn't you say?' And one of them volunteered to take us up there, toot-de-sweet, in his Renault 4.

See? Being Scottish causes magic to happen.

I know you don't believe me about that last, well, if you're not Scottish yourself anyway, so let me prove it.

In 1980 a fellow-Arbroathian friend of mine, Frank Smart, went to find fame and fortune in California. Some ten years after arriving, he had done well. He had his own yacht-rigging business at Venice Beach and was basically printing money.

One day he was driving through the desert, miles from nowhere, on a totally deserted road, with nothing but sand, tumbleweed, blue sky and vultures in sight, when he spotted a lonely figure by the roadside, through the shimmering heat haze.

It's not at all recommended to be out in the open in conditions like that; so Frank dutifully pulled over.

'Can I give you a lift?'

'Aye, please.' quoth the stranger, climbing in. He was a young man, maybe 20.

'Scottish?' asks Frank, recognising his accent.

'Aye. From Arbroath.'

'Arbroath? Gosh. You know, you could die out in the desert like that.'

'Aye, I know, but my last lift turned off there.'

'Where are you going?'

'Venice.'

'Really? Why?'

'Oh, I've got an address for a guy there, Frank Smart. He comes from Arbroath too. My sister went to school with him.' (True. Frank will back me up.)

So you see, the universe focusses its magic on us and causes such things to be. You might call it serendipity or even coincidence; we know better.

Anyway, being Scottish, twenty, and knowing that the universe would look after us, we had omitted to tell our friend Daniel that we might drop by; and being French, twenty, and knowing what Scottish people are like, he just shrugged and said 'Oh, it's okay. We don't have a spare room but you can sleep in the loft.'

For which we were as grateful as had he offered us the presidential suite at the Astoria (or whatever.) So simple life is at that age. Really.

The point of all this is that we were, naturally, invited for dinner *en famille* that evening with Daniel, his parents and sundry. There were two surprises waiting for us. On introduction to Daniel's father, communication was zero. I mean, my French was bad but it wasn't that bad. Not blank look and incomprehension bad. Daniel took me by the elbow. 'It's okay, it's not you. Papa isn't very good in French.'

I must have looked as baffled as I felt, because he laughed. 'This is Brittany, Rod. It's not really France. Most people here speak nothing other than Breton. I mean they learned French at school but they don't use it. So they forget.'

This turned out to be as true as it was surprising and I immediately began to ask questions of myself. After all, as you will have noticed, I am proud to be a Celt but back then I couldn't even manage to say *'Coire Dearg'* without sounding like an Englishman. (And if you just heard 'Coyre Dee-argh' then you know what I mean.) And here I was, a mere two hundred miles from Paris, and not a word of French was being spoken in the house we had been welcomed into.

As the hour waxed towards eating, more and more sons of the soil appeared. They looked surprisingly like the ones in P'tit Moulin, and I guess farmers everywhere.

We sat, in the flagged kitchen, on long benches at a table that was fully ten feet long and we had to squeeze in. There were maybe twenty people there all in. Daniel's mother and sister appeared, handing out the covers – a fork, a spoon (wooden) and a plate. I wondered why there was no knife and the half-formed question was answered as all the other dinner guests reached into their pockets and pulled out their Opinels.

'Oh, wait,' exclaimed Daniel. 'You don't have knives?'

We shook our heads like the dumbest of beasts.

'Don't worry, we have a couple of spares.'

So we were spared the embarrassment of having to cut the meat with a wooden spoon, but it was an eye-opener, you know. I had already experienced culture shock, in large doses, when I had travelled to India the year before, so I knew what it was like. And here I was in the heart of

Croutons and Cheese!

a great modern European nation, being culturally shocked to the core, surrounded by people who only spoke Breton and whose habits were surprisingly different.

Anyway, that's where I learned to mop the plate with the bread between each course. When you think about it, there's nothing uncivilised about it, and it's even green, cutting down on all that nasty detergent.

We also learned of the favourite tipples of the Breton – cider and calvados. But more of that another time; safe to say, by the time we toddled off to bed you could have thrown us in the ditch and we'd have slept like babies.

We didn't, because while getting there was hazy, we woke up, to a golden morning of sunshine, on the palliasses in the loft – which, by the way, turned out to be above the cowshed. But it was summer and they were out.

Les Stephans

When we first moved to P'tit Moulin we spent a great amount of time researching all the junk dealers and scrap-yards, as one does, when one moves to a foreign land. Amongst the first we found was just at the entrance to the nearest town. It was run by a crusty little man of indeterminate age, who had several very large dogs who were a lot less friendly than he was.

If any of my readers are Scots and are familiar with the legendary Sammy Burns' yard outside Edinburgh, then they know pretty much what this place was like. It was really just a field, filled with ancient caravans, vehicles – mostly vans – old sheds and makeshift shelters. Most of them were being overtaken by nature as the vegetation, at least in summer, grew up around them, and they all had that green patina that comes from years in the open.

Inside these was the stock and this was remarkable.

There seemed no limit to the owner's eclecticism. Every dilapidated van or makeshift shelter was crammed to the roof. There was everything to be had here, from oil paintings to sabots, tap fittings to saws. There were huge wheeled trucks that had come from the old mines, filled to the top with tools of every description – and of course you could only see the very top layers.

There were caravans jammed full of bicycles and did I mention sabots? One was absolutely crammed with them, hundreds, maybe more, pairs – and all of them full of woodworm. The paintings were set on end like books on a bookshelf, jammed together so that you had to ease them out to see them. Nearly all were damaged in some way, by dampness and exposure and most of the frames were falling apart.

Naturally, *le patron* considered his wares all to be precious antiques, but at least he was open to negotiation. As so often in France, there are protocols to observe, and only a fool forgets them So let me explain.

You are not going to be mistaken for a French person. That means you must be a foreigner. This is not racism; Parisians are, by definition, not French either. But since you are not a Parisian and everyone knows this, then, as an identified *étranger*, you fit certain classifications, which go something like this:

Swiss; stratospherically rich, incredibly stupid. May be rude, depending on whether Francophone or not. Will buy any old junk at ridiculous prices.

German; even more rich and stupid as well as being infernally rude, and parsimonious with it. The self-appointed European master-race who must ever be reminded that while we are allies now, we were not always. Inclined to talk at the top of their voices over everyone else.

Dutch; incomprehensible in any language. Like the Germans but on the right side. Less parsimonious but only slightly less rude.

Belgian; thick as mince, will buy anything at ridiculous prices, may safely be mocked. Even when insulted they remain polite. The worst drivers on Earth, keep a safe distance when they are near anything that might pass for a vehicle.

Swedes and other Scandinavians; who?

Italians, Spanish, Portuguese, Greeks; all the same. They never buy anything anyway and are incomprehensible. Speak Romance languages but can't be bothered to learn proper French.

Canadian: Like the real French but a bit more thick. Very wealthy indeed. They speak French that hasn't been spoken here in centuries but think they can chatter away like locals. But at least they are Francophone, unlike the ones who haven't even learned French; they just get lumped in with the next lot.

Which brings us to you, my dear reader, because you are unquestionably Anglophone, and so you are '*Anglais*'. It doesn't matter whether you come from Missouri, New South Wales or Brighton, or for that matter Winnipeg, you're *Anglais* and that is that.

Which makes you: not very bright. Prepared to buy anything at silly prices, but inclined to be cheap and pretend to have no money. However you are not as rich as the Swiss or the Germans, so you can be looked down on a bit.

You deserted the French at Dunkirk and will never be allowed to forget it, even though you came back four years later; after all, you have a history of being the 'enemy', *n'est-ce pas?*

Your most recent offence to the Glorious Republic was when you voted to leave the European Union, for which thou shalt surely pay, and dearly.

You are naturally very rude but not nearly as much as the Germans. Your French is atrocious and it is not impolite to laugh at it. You don't understand bargaining, famously, and will just pay whatever is asked. If you do bargain, you do it badly and always lose.

Now there is one way out of this dilemma, but you English can't use it, nor can the Yanks, the Canucks, the Ozzies or the Kiwis (who?).

This extremely useful get-out-of-jail-free card is only available to those of us from that wonderful northern paradise, Scotland, the glorious Western jewel of Ireland, or the idiosyncratic, waterlogged but delightful land of the valleys, Wales. (And no, just because your great-great-great-grand-daddy came from Ullapool does not mean you're Scottish. Harsh, I know, but that is the way it is.)

'Oh why is this?' you complain vociferously.

Because, dear reader, we are not *Anglais*. We are *Celtes*. And that makes *all* the difference.

Now I freely admit that I only speak a few words of Gaelic, but that's doing better than most of my compatriots, who can't even pronounce the names of mountains in their own country properly, thanks to an education system that glorifies English and specifically attempts to eradicate all other indigenous tongues; but you see, your modern French person doesn't actually speak Gaulish either – for very similar reasons. What is it with imperialist cultures? So insecure.

Anyway that means we are on safe ground to say '*Ciamar a tha?*

Chan eil Gaidhlig acam ach beacan, och aye the noo and it's a braw bricht moonlicht nicht the nicht, kilty kilty cauld-dowp, the De'il's awa wi the Exciseman and Donald whaur's yer troosers,' and the Frogs will fall about in raptures. And those of my compatriots who actually do have God's language, well, you will be fêted, and the same applies to the Irish – the ones who paid attention at school – or the Welsh, many of whom really do speak Gaulish. It's not called *'Pays de Gauls'* for nothing, you know.

Then, slip into the French person's brain some half-remembered twaddle about Mary Queen of Scots and the Auld Alliance, not to mention a haunted castle or three, and we are talking serious turkey here. Long lost brother stuff, even...well, sometimes, especially if the person you are talking to is Breton. In this case you are guaranteed the best price in town, probably a few drams on the strength too and in all likelihood an invitation for dinner. I am not making this up.

I'm sure the Welsh do something similar with leeks and harps and the Irish with leprechauns.

So I always make sure they know, right up front, where I come from. In fact I routinely wear a kilt or tartan trews so that I can, with a flourish, say, 'Of course I'm Scottish; look.'

It makes negotiations so much easier. But it's not available to everyone.

Anyway back to these yards. That editor of mine can be so strict.

These fascinating places, half salvage-yard, half tip, are found all over France, and something you may not know is that most of them are owned by one family. Now I don't mean some sort of Mafia-like clan with a boss of bosses at the head, smuggling wormy clogs to China; but they are mostly of the same family, and that's why they are known throughout France as 'Les Stephans'.

Apparently they came from eastern Europe; nobody is sure quite when. Some say they came from Romania after the War (though we are not sure which one) others that, yes they came from around there, but it was much longer ago.

They quickly established themselves as rag and bone men – dealers in 'mungo' and 'jerry'. Anyone old enough to remember the UK's rag and bone men, or even *Steptoe and Son,* the wonderful sitcom based on them, starring Wilfrid Brambell and Harry H. Corbett, will know exactly what I'm talking about.

The fact is that the Stephans themselves even look like the fictional *Steptoe and Son*, and although they now drive around in small open trucks rather than horses and carts, very little has changed.

It's easy, in our throwaway society, to belittle the importance of people like these. Indeed, we are conditioned to, from youth. But before recycling yards there were mungo and jerry merchants, the rag and bone men, the Stephans, and they all provided that essential service that any urbanised society requires: to take away what we have bought and used but no longer desire or have need of and sell it to those who do desire and need it but have not the wherewithal to buy new. And for doing so they take a meagre crust.

The fact is that people have been doing this since the dawn of civilisation and we should not mock them, for their lifestyle oils the wheels of our culture. They may appear somewhat unorthodox, and do not neatly check the boxes that idiot bureaucrats, nosy tax officers or authoritarian (and racist) policemen like to see checked; but we should never forget that these functionaries, like it or not, actually work for *us*. Which includes the Stephans and all the others like them.

We could not pretend, even if we wanted to, that the Stephans were precise adherents of the laws that ordinary mortals are forced to succumb to; but that doesn't make their life easy.

A beautiful example would be the number of times I drove past our local Stephan's yard on a freezing winter's morning – for it can get cold here in the Arrière-côte – the rime thick on the ground and whitening everything. I would often see a black pillar of smoke rising from the centre and there, by it, our Stephan, warming his old bones over a fire made of coils of electric cables from which he was burning the insulation, in order to separate the copper. You get a good price for copper.

This was the life he had: on the one hand far harder than most of us would accept, yet on the other, more free than most could aspire to. And yes, laws and ordinances were broken, as witnessed by the plumes of acrid black smoke swirling around him.

I think the idea was that the *caporal* permanently fixed to his lower lip was so noxious that it made all other airborne toxins admit defeat.

Although our old Stephan retired and gave up his yard many years ago now, I am very happy to say that we have not lost these stalwarts of the market economy.

The other source of the used, cheap and intriguing, is Emmaüs. This is a charity set up by the Abbé Pierre, in 1954, to try to provide shelter for the homeless. It works in a very simple and efficient manner. Emmaüs buys up old properties cheaply and turns them over to homeless people, who are organised by a team of social workers. Locals donate unwanted goods, which the charity then sells. Part of the money so earned goes to wards renovating the property and providing decent housing, and part is returned the centre where it is used to fund new projects. There is, I believe, even an Emmaüs in England these days.

Well, from what we see from here, they probably need one.

Think of Emmaüs as being like a thrift shop on steroids; all your UK High Street charity shops rolled into one.

There is one big difference, however. Whereas almost none of the money earned from the treasures you donate to charities in the UK ever actually gets used to fund the projects they advertise, most of the money Emmaüs makes goes directly not just to helping the poor and needy, but to the specific project where the sales occur. That is because it is only *after* the money the project needs is found, that any surplus goes to the centre.

We could probably wax rhetoric about how, once again, the British couldn't organise a piss-up in a brewery and no other nation (sic) could possibly consider it 'normal' for over 90% of the funds raised by a charity to go to its own bureaucracy -- and remember, mark you, that nearly all the staff are working for free. But I believe some people don't like it when I carry on like that so I shall say no more.

Suffice to say that Emmaüs is the favourite shop of most everyone I know. Combined salvage yard and thrift shop, it is a wonder. And amazing what one finds there. Really.

Wine, Bread and Camembert

Last week I was waiting in the queue at the supermarket when I fell into conversation with a particular.

He was tall, thin, a full head of white of hair, had not shaved in several days, sported a voluminous moustache and his clothes were... comfortable. And had been so for quite some time.

His purchases for the day?

A loaf of bread, a bottle of wine and a Camembert.

'Are you married?' he demanded. (It's okay, don't worry.)

'No,' I replied, honestly. 'I used to be. Divorced.'

A slow smile cracked his features, revealing a dentition that resembled a view of the Western Cemetery in my home town.

'Ah, good, good, that's the way,' quoth he. 'Women are just trouble.' He held up his purchases. 'This is all a man needs. And cigarettes.'

I refrained from telling him I had a girlfriend and didn't smoke; best not to spoil his pleasure.

Oh, to be so innocently unreconstructed. It transpired that his lunch was, and had been, for over forty years, a loaf, a cheese and a bottle of wine, followed up by a *caporal*.

'And I'm seventy-eight,' he cackled.

I have to admit, it did seem to be suiting him.

For me, alas, the genes are against it. The consequence of such a lifestyle is an immediate spread of the waistline which ends in me not being able to get into any of my clothes and having to diet. Which I hate. I did consider taking up smoking, having heard that this kept the weight down, but a few pictures of the inside of smokers' lungs was enough to settle that particular hash.

I am reminded of my old friend and mentor, Stanley Hunter, 'Thirty-nine years on the Daily Express and don't you forget it!' Once, when we were just digesting an excellent lunch back at the newsroom of Scotland on Sunday, one of the Features editorial staff (the 'limp-wristed bastards' according to Mr H.) flounced over with a request for photographs he hoped we might condescend to provide. Stan was the boss so I let him deal with it.

'Aye, okay,' he said, to the limp-wristed one's amazement. (It were alway wise to ask such things of Stan in the hour after lunch, when the warm glow of a fine repast was still warming the cockles of his heart. Or something.)

'Golfing this evening, Stanley?' I think it was an attempt at diplomacy; it was March and unless you have luminous balls (not those ones, you idiot) golf is hard in the dark. And lest ye doubt the existence of luminous golf balls, I have the pictures to prove they do. True.

'No. I am going to have a couple of pints, then eat dinner and have an excellent bottle of wine with it.' (It was Tuesday or Wednesday, I can't remember which; they tend to be slack days on a Sunday paper.)

The other's jaw dropped. 'What, a whole bottle?' Clearly this one did not understand the warning signs. I think he would have been better advised to attempt humour with less unpredictable creatures than long-serving hard news men...like grizzly bears or something.

Stanley slammed the desk; he had a clear space specifically for that, right next to the phone. It was the only part of the desk you could actually see. 'Laddie,' he roared, 'I drink a bottle of wine every night!'

The limp-wristed one turned puce and departed, doubtless to tell the other feckless items of his ilk another story about the terrible monsters that inhabited the Picture Desk. We fell about laughing.[1]

Stanley's prophylactic against the deadly waistline bulge that comes with consuming a thousand calories worth or so of alcohol a day was indeed golf (albeit not in the dark) and we shall discuss this and his adventures on the course, in another book, I shouldn't doubt. But it won't really work in France, because there aren't enough golf courses.

Being a Scot, I am used to golf courses being those damned encumbrances that stop a fellow getting to the beach. I mean there's hardly a mile of the east coast of Scotland that isn't a golf course, a nature reserve, or a three hundred foot cliff. Everybody plays golf. We learn it at school. The damn game was invented in Scotland, I mean, what do you think? Not being able to convincingly address a ball is a confession of failure for a Scot.

In France, however, playing golf is considered snobby and anti-revolutionary. It suggests airs and graces and most of the French do the

---

[1] Stanley is a real person, and one of the most lovely men I have ever had the pleasure of meeting or working with; a mentor, confidant and dear friend.

inverted snobbery thing that bourgeois, comfortable French people are so good at...kind of like when they steal tins of tuna from the supermarket when they have oodles of money to pay for them. It's a part of the national character. The French are at once in awe of the aristocracy, whether hereditary or honorary, the hyper rich and the great bears of politics, and utterly disdainful of anyone who might appear to want to join their ranks or be like them in any way; and golf, my dears, is an establishment sport in France.

Now there's snobbery a-plenty in Scottish golf. The town I grew up in had two clubs, the Arbroath Golf Club and the Arbroath Artisan's Golf Club. The unwashed were expected, by the washed, to join the latter, and they had a selection committee to see that they did. Don't run away with the idea that Scotland is immune from these offensive notions of class, even if they were imported from our dear neighbours to the south.

But in France it's far worse. Here they don't even have an Artisan's Club and the membership fees of the regular ones make Muirfield look cheap.

I like to whack the small balls, although I would be the first to admit I'm not very good; but in my youth I was an okay Sunday player. Golf is dull played alone, but in France, finding a companion to make up a pair is almost impossible, and a foursome? Pigs might fly. Moira, by the way, could never stand golf. I don't think she knows which end of the bat is up. (And that is a specific observation about golf, not a general comment about her mental state. By the way.)

I only once found a regular partner here, a Japanese American who went by the name of Mike Kinjo. He felt exactly as I did, that the French attitude towards this excellent pastime was ridiculous to say the least. There's a nice little nine-holer at Autun, a municipal one with very reasonable green fees at that – or they were back then – and we used to meet up there for a regular couple of rounds – well, nine holes, you know. But since Mike went back to the States I've not been able to find another partner. Any time I dangle the suggestion under the nose of a French bod I get The Look. You know the one.

So the golf sticks moulder in the cupboard under the stairs. Occasionally I take them to the field where once we had a vegetable garden and fire a load of practise shots up the hill to the top. I think it amuses the neighbour's cows and I haven't brained one so far.

French Onion Soup! II

Quite what the Moulinards – the two-legged ones – think of this bizarre behaviour I should not hazard to guess.

A Little History

P'tit Moulin, although the name is a little changed, is a real place and it has a real history. It was originally established by the Gauls, but there is little left of their era now. The Gauls didn't build in stone and no serious excavations have been made.

Gaul before the Romans arrived was a thriving economy, and the reason why P'tit Moulin came to be. It was on a crossroads between four other much more important centres. These were Autun, originally Augustodinum, and Beaune; and Arnay le Duc and Nolay. These were, even two thousand years ago, wealthy and important centres of industry and commerce. Autun and the lands to the east and north-east of P'tit Moulin were, even then, important for the mining of iron ore, which was, in turn, made into manufactured goods of all sorts from agricultural implements to knives and swords and household artefacts.

It's easy for us, with our modern blinkers on, to underestimate the development of Europe two millennia ago. Europe, before the Black Death hit in the fourteenth century, was bustling and prosperous. That is after all, the reason why the Romans were so desperate to conquer it.

The Romans, under Caesar, conquered Gaul in 50 BCE. Oh, who could forget the long, flyblown schooldays studying his self-glorifying account of the conquest, 'De Bello Gallico'. Oh you didn't? Well, you're probably lucky not to have had to struggle with the intricacies of Latin declinations. But it does exist in translation and it's well worth the read if you're a bit of a Francophile like me.

This part of Gaul was Romanised quickly because the local nation, the Eduoen, had signed a peace treaty with Rome before Caesar got uppity, so he was unable to raze the place and take all the inhabitants as slaves, as he was wont to do elsewhere. So it remained prosperous.

One evidence of this is a Gallo-Roman stele, or gravestone, now housed in the church. It shows a wealthy man and woman, doubtless man and wife. The Gauls quickly adopted Roman marriage customs, especially after the introduction of Christianity, which appeared early here. Goddess-worship was the previous religion of the Gauls and this was one of the main reasons why Mary was given such an important role in the Christian tradition.

One of the problems in researching the history of small French towns is that many of the records were destroyed during the Revolution. However, we know that a castle was built here in the 11th century and soon after the present church was built. The chateau is believed by the locals to have been one of the residences of Marguerite, sometimes known as Anne, of Bourgogne. According to local gossip, she was fond of men, and this castle may have been the location for some of her many liaisons. But I can find nothing official that says she was anything other than a typical aristocrat of the era. You may take that as you will.

During the Revolution, the people of P'tit Moulin were Royalists whereas those from Ivry, the next village up, were Revolutionaries. The wife of the village Notary wrote a long explanation of what happened when the men of Ivry came to P'tit Moulin.

First they beat up the men with staves until they were unconscious or dead. They dragged the women to the square in front of the church and tied them to a stake. There they were stripped bare to the waist and then flogged.

Once the Revolutionaries had done with the women they attacked the house of the Notary. Contrary to the Revolutionary laws, the Notary had been conducting marriages and registering births and deaths as well as notarising legal documents – all of which were now the preserve of the Revolutionary authorities.

They broke into the house and arrested the Notary. However they did not ransack his office, but instead sealed it with cords to which they applied wax with the revolutionary seal on. The contents were to be examined by an investigator who would come from Dijon.

Before he was taken away to prison the Notary was able to speak to his wife. If certain documents in his office were discovered, then not only he, but numerous others in the village, would face the *guillotine.*

That night his wife went home and for once the fact that French interior walls are so thin was a benefit. Working from the outside of the partition, she loosened a section of brick and plaster and slipped it out of the way. This allowed her to enter the office without breaking the seals – which would have meant her certain death.

The next day she set off, on foot, for Dijon, where her husband was being held. She carried the documents with her, at great risk to herself. Had she been searched the game would have been up. She was able to show them to her husband in the prison, and he told her which to destroy. On leaving the city she made a fire in the woods and burned them, then hurried home.

The distance from P'tit Moulin to Dijon is around thirty miles, so our woman was not only brave and loyal, but fit and well-shod, for she arrived back in P'tit Mouln before daybreak, where she re-entered the room and replaced the documents – which were now, of course, entirely innocent.

She replaced the documents and re-plastered the wall

After making herself presentable, she waited on the revolutionary investigator, who sure enough, duly arrived, opened the office and took the Notary's legal documents with him.

Since there was now no evidence of wrong-doing, the case against the Notary was dropped and he was released. He served the villagers of P'tit Moulin for many more years, until long after the Terror had abated.

Now my part-time neighbour, Jean-Luc and I had a friendly dispute for many years as to whether it would have been in his house or mine that the brave Notary and his loyal wife lived. I always said that his was the *relais de la poste,* so that ruled that out, and mine was not bourgeois enough. However, fascinatingly, another house nearby came up for sale just recently and after it was bought, as a second home by a Frenchman, I was invited to look around. I was amazed. Far from being a typical country house, here was a real maison bourgeoise, complete with panelled walls in the *grande salle*. It had a balcony, and a beautiful marble fireplace. This intrigued me because the story of the Notary's wife mentions both the balcony – from which the Notary observed the arrival of the Revolutionaries – and a fancy fireplace.

Guess what else? Behind one of the walls, hidden by the panelling, was a small office, with only enough room for a desk and a filing cabinet. It was concealed by one of those false doors that blended into the panelling of the main room. However, to the hallway outside, there's only one thickness of cloison, made of those famous inch-thick French bricks. Could this have been the famous Notary's house? I think it might have been. Jean-Luc is not so sure.

We think of 'post' as having something to do with letters and it does, but this was not the original meaning at all.

Originally, the 'post' was a system of horse-exchange. A horse that is worked hard for one day has to be rested for three. So if you want to go anywhere that is more than a day's hard ride away, you have a problem. You either have to take a three-day break or change horses. I suppose you could just go more slowly, but we still haven't learned to do that.

The 'post' was where the exchange horses were kept. Before the arrival of the canals (you know what I mean) and later the railways, the only means of public transport, and delivery of important communications, was by horse, usually hauling a coach. But the coach can't rattle from Paris to Lyon in one go; it has to go in stages so the horses can be changed. Which is why it's called a stagecoach. I bet you always wondered about that. And of course the mail became the 'Post' because it was carried from post to post by the coaches. You keeping up at the back there?

Anyway, Jean-Luc's house is the old *relais de la poste*, the very horse-changing and resting place we began with.

In the past. P'tit Moulin was on an important crossroads, so it had a rather grand *relais* which was actually built right over the road, like a train station. The road itself went through a vaulted tunnel with platforms on either side for the passengers to alight.

There were bedrooms for them to stay in and of course, a restaurant, for the humans this time, and I am sure the horses were as well taken care of.

Interestingly, this post system is one that those great innovators, the Romans, never came up with, so their mail was transported by runner. Apparently humans can be worked hard till they drop every day without having to be rested; a popular philosophy today. But never mind that, I do believe some readers don't like it when I wax political. Then again, as my dear little Auntie Ruth says, 'Fuckem'. If they don't like it they can write their own...

Now back to the post. The old road then led down the hill through *Rue du Pont*, past the putative Notary's house (and its proximity to the source of communication makes it an even greater likelihood) and away to Nolay and thence onward. Of course, there is no bridge there any more, since the road was widened over a century ago and diverted over the culvert which, if you recall, was the source of that little annoyance with Monsieur Rey's cows being up to their udders in *la merde*.

So nowadays, Rue du Pont is a distinctly sleepy little street with precious little in the way of action, save for the colony of cats that inhabit one of the *caves*. But it must have been impressive enough in the 18th century, with the *diligence* (French for stagecoach) rattling off south or arriving with tired passengers and long awaited mails, scattering chickens and followed by barking dogs and children. I mean the dogs were barking, you see?

Now even the main road is little used; it was replaced by what used to be called the N6 and then by a spanking shiny motorway, the A6, the *Autoroute de Soleil*. Life in P'tit Moulin is no longer interspersed with such excitements as it once was. The N6, by the way, though now downgraded, still exists and is still one of the great routes of France, a real driver's delight, especially for motorcyclists. Not to be missed.

For *aficionados* of history, P'tit Moulin and its surrounding area is a wonderland of exploration. Not far away, between Beaune and Chagny, is a reconstructed Gaulish village of the type that would have been here. I was struck, looking at it, how similar the houses were to the ccrannogs of my native Scotland. These were large wooden, thatched houses built on piers over lochs, where they were not only more defensible, but benefited from a natural form of sanitary disposal. And fish for the table; though the juxtaposition might be less than appetising to us!

There are echoes of the Roman era everywhere. Nearby is Cussy la Colonne, where there is a third-century Gallo-Roman column measuring 11.6 metres in height, possibly venerating Hercules. This is a very rare artefact indeed and I am surprised that it is not more highly promoted. *Monuments de France* must have other things to do.

On the other hand, I remember once, many years ago, driving on my trusty Norton 850 Commando from Kent, right across the south of England to Devon, where I had spent a halcyon summer the year before. I had been working the hop harvest and my hip pocket was satisfyingly replete. Now I was following the scent of the West Wind – and, coincidentally you understand, a young lady.

Not even realising where I was, as I traversed a green plain of undulating grassland, I came across an assembly of huge stones stood on end, just by the road. I stopped and dismounted; it was evening and the low light glanced the megaliths and gilded them. I wandered around, amazed, and alone. There was not a soul there other than me.

It was a moment of reflection and peace that I remember even now.

I am an atheist but a spiritual one and I know how close I was to my Mother, the Earth, on that distant evening. I have felt that closeness often and revel in it. I know I shall one day sleep in her bosom again.

But today, I could not do that. Stonehenge – as it was – has long been encircled by a fence. It is open during appropriate hours only and a fee is charged to do as I did; and one could never be alone there, not now, alone with the Goddess and the soughing wind, as the evening sun reddened.

So maybe the French are right to do as they do; to leave their monuments open. This is France; nobody daubs them with graffiti or chips off bits for souvenirs. Here, one can still be part of the distant past of humanity without the intrusion of crass modernity and the clunking tills of capitalism.

Not far from here there used to be a nunnery. It was just on the Vallée de l'Ouche. It was a lovely place and while the abbé and outbuildings themselves were closed to the public, the gardens were open, and what lovely gardens they were. We had many a happy day there when the children were young. Indeed a picture taken there is the front cover of the first book in this series, *French Onion Soup!*

We have so many memories of that place and all of them good. For over a hundred years, the gardens had been open to the public and patronised by them; children had played within the safety of its walls and mothers and grandmothers chatted in the shade of its trees.

Then, a few years ago, something awful happened. The sisters gave up the convent and sold it to an *Anglais*. Well, this wasn't a real *Anglais*, he was one of those USican ones, but it comes to the same thing, at least in France.

Naturally, being a USican, this item could see no point in anything he could not grub some money out of, so he promptly turned the convent into a hotel. That was fair enough, but to the horror of all his neighbours, he closed the gardens and reserved them for guests.

I am told the restaurant there is very good, but nobody I know has ever been to find out. It is a rumour they have heard, though in fact, they don't know anyone who has actually eaten there either. But yes; it is 'very good'. I haven't been and I don't plan to go. I think it would be bad form; even in a world almost bled dry by the scourge of USican capitalism, we are not yet on our knees. There is such a thing as decency.

Croutons and Cheese!

Whenever I pass, however, I do stop by the gate so I can piss on it. Frenchness is very catching.

When I was told about this catastrophe by Antoine *le Potier*, he did not explicitly say, 'only an *Anglais* could have done something so utterly boorish' but that's what he thinks and he's right. So I am not telling you the name of this place, lest you be tempted to patronise it; you can do your research and doubtless you might locate it, but at least it won't be my fault.

So indeed, perhaps the French have the right of it; they leave their monuments and public places open and even the great cathedrals are free to visit, though a coin or two in the box is always appreciated. But it is voluntary and it makes the soul feel good. If we have to pay at the gate, then the first thing in our minds is 'was it worth the money?'

A propos of the USican, there is something that, in a lifetime of travel, I have always believed and if anything more deeply now than at any time in the past.

It is that when you go to another country, you must respect the way things are there. I have never had any trouble when travelling, because I have always respected the local ways and treated the local people with courtesy. This is something that, I am afraid, many others seem never to learn. By no means all are USicans, but it is a lesson they in particular would do well to learn. The example of the boor who closed the gardens to people whose families had been using them for generations is a telling one. He had no respect for those who lived there; he was only interested in multiplying his money. I shouldn't expect to be well liked with an attitude like that.

Then again, not all USicans are detested. There was, once, a tall lady from Georgia (the American one) who lived close to Ivry. Her husband was French and she seemed to have, in general, a pretty good understanding of the *modus vivandi*. I remember meeting her at a village Christmas party. Her eyes widened when she realised I was another *Anglais*, and this time a 'British' one.

'Hello,' she said. She was a good 5'10" and by any measure an attractive woman, so she did have my attention. 'Tell me something,' she pursued, *sotto voce*, 'Do you really call those things *baubles?*' I confess my mind must have been drifting. For a moment there I was thinking of something else altogether and was umm, somewhat at a loss for a reply, until I realised she was gesticulating towards an ornately decorated Christmas tree.

'Baubles? Oh yes,' I gasped, somewhat in relief. I mean Moira was only a few feet away. 'Yes, we do. What do you call them?'

'Christmas decorations,' she replied, looking at me as if I were mad. Which I probably am.

I was interested to note the effect she had on the French men around me. She spoke very good, grammatically correct French, but with an accent that you could have cut with a knife, even to my ear. I mean French with a Southern States twang is quite different from the way they speak in P'tit Moulin.

I quizzed Antoine about this later. 'Yes, she's beautiful,' he sighed, waxing rhapsodic. 'And her voice!'

'Her voice?'

'*Mon Dieu*, it's so *sexy*,' he exclaimed, and then shook himself.

It would appear that French men find the accent of *une Anglaise* (especially, it seems, one from south of the Mason-Dixon) speaking in French to be heart-meltingly romantic. Apparently it has the same effect that Sophie Marceau has on me when she speaks in English. (And no, I will never forgive Christophe Lambert for snagging her, even if it do seem uncharitable.)

The Boys Next Door

The house next door used to be owned by a very interesting group of particulars. We were forewarned of their existence in somewhat hushed tones by one of the other neighbours, who kept passing amused glances towards their house. They were *'tres sympa'*. We were not to be afraid of them. They were quite harmless. Positively sweet, once you got to know them.

Quite honestly these reassurances were terrifying. What were these people? Serial murderers? Who on earth needs *that* much positive publicity?

I had been long enough in France to know that the phrase *'tres sympa'* can have a multitude of meanings, so my curiosity was piqued. However, as the particulars actually lived in Paris and only visited during the holidays, I could do little more in the way of investigation. So I did what I always do and asked Antoine *le Potier,* next time we got together for *aperos.*

'Ah, yes, the boys,' he intoned, sucking a tooth. 'They're homosexuals.'

'Cool,' I replied. I went to art school. There is very little in the way of human sexuality that I find shocking. Antoine was visibly relieved.

'I am glad. You never know. Some people are not very accepting, around here.' And then he proceeded to give me the low-down.

It turned out there were three of them, Gaston, Jean-Pierre and François. That was where it stopped being simple.

Apparently Gaston was the eldest of the three. He had bought the house twenty years before as a weekend retreat. He took the then young, blonde and beautiful Jean-Pierre as his lover. Gaston's previous love and partner had retired and decamped for Tangiers, which is the go-to location for older French men with a taste for...cute young men.

Tangiers was the Pattaya of the late nineteenth century, a place rich with sleaze and cheap sex. Did you know that Oscar Wilde and Albert Camus became firm friends while chasing Arab boys there? Well then, you learn something new every day. Anyway, while Tangiers has lost its appeal, apparently, for the Anglophone fancier of 'bottoms like two plums in a sock', it remains highly regarded amongst French-speaking *aficionados* of the delicacy.

Jean-Pierre duly bought out Gaston's previous partner and became a half share holder in the house next door to us. Are you keeping up?

Well, time went by and Gaston got older; and so did Jean-Pierre. We are not quite sure who got too old for whom, but it turned out that Gaston too was taking more and more breaks in Tangiers, while Jean-Pierre had landed himself a new fish, in the form of François.

François was a little different from the other two. He was certainly beautiful, but he had no interest in the catering business. He was distinctly upper-crust, in the way that the French do it; it's just a little more stylish. And being gay probably helped. He was an alumnus of one of the *Grandes Ecoles* – the French equivalent of Oxbridge.

He had entered the Diplomatic Corps, where he was, he told us in the most unassuming way, guaranteed a stellar career. I am not sure whether this was because of or despite his obvious homosexuality. In another milieu and with the application of modern hormone and surgical techniques, François could have been a very beautiful woman. He was blonde and petite and had remarkable blue eyes.

Anyway, because François had no interest in the cafe he did not buy out Gaston's share of that or the house. So we were left with a *ménage a trois*.

This had somewhat confused the locals, although, to their credit, they took it well. I think they might have been more resistant to a group of three local men setting up home together, but Parisians? Well, everyone knows they are beyond comprehension.

We met the famed *ménage* – all three of them – that August, during the usual mass annual break.

Gaston and Jean-Pierre were dog-lovers. Unfortunately, they were lovers of that breed of rats masquerading as canines, Yorkshire Terriers. I have a deep love of dogs, but these things would best serve as footballs if you ask me. And I don't mean the American kind.

Despite this grotesque flaw, the 'boys' were a very pleasant and gracious triad, even if one could not help but wonder how exactly the relationship worked out, sexually.

All three were very aware of the effect they had on the village. Gaston was not at all effeminate and basically was a straight man who liked young men. François, although somewhat less convincing, also affected masculinity. Jean-Pierre, on the other hand, was flaming.

I have never had an issue with highly effeminate gay men. I don't find them in the least threatening and generally, they are great fun, good company, have brilliant senses of humour and a mischievous sarcasm that is a marvel to behold. So it was with Jean-Pierre. Once he figured out that a) I was straight and b) I was cool with the fact that he wasn't, he did that 'best female friend' thing that only effeminate gay men know how to do...and it was hilarious. His teasing was never offensive and always on the right side of propriety – just. Since Moira and I had met at art school and moved in the same crowd, which contained a lot of gay and gender non-conforming people, she knew I was relaxed with this. She even told the boys, which only made Jean-Pierre worse.

He reserved his most delectable torment, however, for the locals. Jean-Pierre, while very feminine in his comportment, when relaxing with friends, was a conventional dresser who affected a straight character when in public; I have known a few French gay men like this and I think it's to do with the social climate.

However, for the benefit of his audience in P'tit Moulin, he used to put on a show every morning that literally silenced the crowd.

At that time, *Chez Angèle* was busy from dawn to dusk, and breakfast was no different, with the local imbibers, the stalwart and horny-handed sons of the soil, stocking up on wine and *crêpe*s for the day ahead...well, till lunchtime anyway. Towards the end of their session, around nine-thirty, our man would put on the show,

Dressed in nothing (apparently) other than a silk kimono and a pair of boudoir slippers, he would flounce his way to *Chez Angèle*. Before he entered, the hubbub would, as usual, be plainly audible from our kitchen. The instant he walked in – silence. It would stay silent till he left, usually flirting most outrageously with Madame *la patronne* and clutching his packs of *Marlboro*. As he walked back across the road he was heading towards our kitchen and every morning he had a grin on that would shame the Cheshire Cat.

Unfortunately, in the end, the *ménage* collapsed. I understand that François was posted overseas. The relationship continued for a while but then he struck up with a senior member of the Diplomatic Corps and moved on, leaving Jean-Pierre heart-broken. Gaston had always been tied to France because of his father, who needed regular kidney dialysis. In the end, he passed, and Gaston had no further impediment to spending most of his time in Tangiers enjoying the company of those brown-skinned boys.

With the three now so divided, there was nought for it but to sell;

and that they did. The partnership in the cafe and the house was divided and as far as I know, Jean-Pierre continued in business with another associate. Whether this was allied to a romantic liaison I could not tell you.

I miss them. They were the best kind of neighbours; polite and welcoming and great with the kids. Never once did they hesitate to lend a hand if we needed it and they always refused to take anything in return, although we shared many fine dinners together. But *c'est la vie*. The world turns.

African Market

P'tit Moulin is about half an hour's drive from Chalon sur Saone, a city I have always been very fond of. Chalon has a wonderful French Market three days a week, and you will be flat amazed at the selection of things available.

However, and unknown to many visitors, there is another market in Chalon, in one of the suburbs, called Champforgeiul.

This is in the middle of an immigrant enclave, which originally, when we first began going in the early 1990s, was a mix of everyone from the old French Empire. There were West Africans, North Africans, Asians, West Indians and Pacific Islanders, alongside the indigenous French. This made it an amazing place to visit, with goods from all over the world.

You could find the best olives from north Africa and herbs and spices to make your head spin. The best *merguez* I have ever tasted come from one of the butchers – and there are two others almost as good. Roast chickens north African style, smelling to make your mouth water from the car park and served with spicy sauce and *'patates'*. African bread that you don't see anywhere else. Fruit and vegetables there were – and are – amazing and ridiculously cheap. I used to get a whole tray of apricots or peaches for ten francs – £1 – and even today the prices are rock-bottom. But beware, the fruit, toothsome and succulent as it is, has to be eaten quickly because it will not keep long.

In other markets, today, the fruit is often hard and unripe and French supermarkets – once a delight for fruit and vegetables – have fallen to the English disease – perfectly shaped specimens that look great, taste of nothing at all, and that you could play *pétanque* with.

But even now at Champforgeiul you can still get the most wonderful fruit and vegetables. Okay, perhaps they're not quite as regular in size and shape. But they do have that essential so completely absent from supermarket fare – flavour – in surpassing amounts.

It was – and remains – a great place to buy clothes. In the 90s and the early 00s, many of the stalls were run by jet black West Africans from Senegal, Niger and other parts. The women wore brilliantly-coloured robes and turbans and the men often had fearsome tribal scarring. Even to my ear they had a pronounced accent; goodness knows what they thought of mine, but we seemed to get along.

I remember once being advised by friends, on hearing that we were planning a trip to this – known to all and sundry as 'the African Market' – to be very careful because it was full of thieves and pickpockets. I was duly forewarned and not unduly concerned: the indigenous French have a deep mistrust of non-indigenous populations – including 'les Anglais'.

One of the stalls we visited on that day was run by an enormous West African with an accent as thick as soup. He was selling Hawaiian shirts, in bright print patterns. I have always been a sucker for shirts like that (to the great distress of several women in my life) and expressed an interest.

Of course, this is the very last thing one should ever do. Being an experienced traveller in the Middle and Far East I should have known better. But I forgot. The shirts – which were cotton print – were marked at 150 francs, or fifteen quid each, and I said no at that.

Very quickly, I was being offered two for 150. That was still steep and it came down, after much gesticulation and huge smiles, to 100 the two. Moira was growing impatient and I turned to leave, and suddenly the price was 50 (a fiver) for two. I couldn't resist that, so I had them, and after profuse handshakes and blessings, bade farewell to my new life-long friend and went to join the family.

As we wandered back through the crowd towards the car park, I became aware of a tumult behind me and turned to see a 6'6 (two metres to you decimalophiles) jet-black man-mountain wearing a Hawaiian shirt as big as a tent careering through the serried shoppers towards me.

It was of course, my new found friend, and as he drew up, his grin lit up the surroundings like the great light at Pharos. (You do know what Pharos was, don't you? It was the lighthouse at the mouth of the port of Alexandria, one of the wonders of the Ancient World.)

I was a little surprised that he had become so attached so quickly, but it was not as I thought. He began waving my wallet under my nose.

'You left this, monsieur,' he exclaimed. 'Is not good!'

He then insisted that I check the contents, which I did, before delivering a stern lecture about how I must never ever do a thing like that again, because the market was full of thieves and vagabonds who would rob me blind in an instant.

Once he was satisfied that I had understood and would never be so careless in the future, he pumped my hand for a good thirty seconds, nearly blinding me with his searchlight grin, and then headed off to his

Croutons and Cheese!

stall, good deed done for the day.

Meanwhile, Moira was busy crying with laughter.

It is as it always is; one tends to have in return, what one gives. I try to treat people as if they are really nice, decent individuals and it is an amazing thing, you know, nearly everyone I meet is; polite, decent and welcoming. Yet I frequently meet others who, by their lights, meet no-one but the most delinquent and disreputable, not to mention downright rude and inhospitable.

I personally think it has something to do with perspective.

The African Market at Champforgeiul is still there (Thursday mornings only, be there sharp) but it has lost much of the variety that made it so fascinating. The West Africans have disappeared; apparently they have moved to Paris or Lyon. There have been fewer and fewer East Asians for ten years now and their little stalls selling Buddhas and other trinkets have all gone. The West Indians, too, have left for pastures new and of smiling Pacific Islanders there is not one to be seen. All that remains are the ubiquitous North Africans – who still have wonderful olives and *merguez* – and the locals with their amazing fruit and veg. It is a shadow of the place it once was, but it is still well worth a visit.

Green Poo

Once, we were living back in Scotland and just visiting our dream house in France whenever we could. When my daughter Cait was very small, Moira stayed at home with her and I took the boys. Cait couldn't really stand the long journey and she was too young to appreciate France; and it gave Moira a far easier time of it, having all four of her male children out of the house for a few weeks. It was always a fun time, but travelling with Sandy, then, was an interesting experience.

In those days you could still get a hovercraft across the Channel, so just for a laugh and to show the boys what it was like, I booked a crossing on one. Naturally they didn't pay any attention to it and just got on with listening to metal music through the headphones. I can't remember if there were iPods then. Sandy bought one of those huge beakers of Coke with some of his holiday money, and I warned him to be careful.

Before we got off the hovercraft, I took the boys – it was just Calum and Sandy – to the bathroom. Sandy didn't want a pee. He can be difficult that way, and he was clearly in one of his 'I'm ignoring everything you say and just doing my thing' moods. So, unable to physically pick him up and wring it out of him, I had to go with it and while Calum dutifully unloaded, Sandy did not and went on sucking on his Coke, despite my dire warnings..

Naturally, the trouble began on the infamous stretch of *autoroute* just outside Calais. It's murderously fast, busy and there is no hard shoulder or security lane, or there wasn't then.

Suddenly I heard from the back seat the dreaded – and predicted – wail: I NEED A PEE!

Dang, there was a surprise.

It was unsafe to pull over and it was obvious from his antics – I could see in the mirror that his face was bright red and he was clutching his groin – that crisis was imminent. I could hardly get him to pee out the window, no matter how much I would have liked to – little perisher. So I was on the point of telling him to do it on the car floor and I would deal with it later, when Calum came to the rescue. He was also in the back with Sandy, watching the proceedings with undisguised horror. He has a bit of a thing about uncontained body fluids in his immediate vicinity.

'It came out of this, so it should go back in!' he exclaimed, holding up the coke pitcher. So Sandy got his pecker out and relieved himself into it. Very carefully, after the emergency had been averted, the boys got the lid back on the pitcher and propped it up in the foot well.

I stopped at the next available *aire* or rest area to empty it. I can now attest that a litre of Coke can be processed by a child's body and piddled out again, nearly filling the receptacle it came in, within half an hour.

We laughed about it. But from then on, when we travelled, we always took a couple of resealable containers with us, just in case.

That was a summer break and it was very hot that year. We liked to go to the market at Nolay on Mondays. It's not a big one but there are a few nice stalls selling cheese and vegetables…it is France. But the main attraction is the pizza stall. It's run by a lovely lady whom we have got to know well over the years and are very fond of. She has a big green van with a real wood-fired oven and her pizzas are absolutely to die for.

She makes them to order and we always go for a drink while we're waiting. It's open road back up to P'tit Moulin so I was relaxed when Sandy ordered a *'diabolo menthe'* which is lemonade with a bright green, minty syrup in it. It does look spectacular.

We drank our drinks, paid up, got the pizzas and headed for home, where we had them under the brolly at the table in the courtyard.

And that was that. Nothing exciting happened.

The fun was the next day.

I was pottering down in the kitchen – in those days it was in the back room – when I heard a bloodcurdling scream from upstairs.

'DADDY!!'

I dropped everything and ran. The horror was taking place in the en-suite bathroom to the master bedroom. When I got there I was confronted with the sight of Calum, ending himself with hysteria on the floor and basically incoherent. Sandy was sitting on the throne with door open and pants down, in the very opposite emotion, tears streaming down his face. He was obviously terrified and for a while there I thought there was an oversized tarantula or something in there with him. Well, we do get big spiders in P'tit Moulin.

But there seemed to be no physical threat at all.

'What's the matter?' I asked, but Sandy was in way too much of a mess to answer.

'It's...it's his *poo*,' managed Calum, between thoroughly unhelpful paroxysms of laughter. 'Look.'

'His poo?'

I looked past the rascal's skinny little backside, expecting the bowl to be full of blood or half-eaten Lego.

But it wasn't. What it was full of was bright green poo. I mean iridescent. Cobalt Green even. Positively fluorescent so it was.

'What the...?'

'It's the *diabolo menthe*,' choked Calum, slowly recovering his composure. 'It must be.' And then he collapsed again.

He was right, and I averted a heart attack. Poor wee Sandy was just looking at me, tears running down his face and his jaw quivering that way children do when they can't cry any more.

I have to say I burst out laughing too. Fortunately, the scamp who'd caused the panic, now reassured, saw the amusing side too.

Once we had cleared up and recovered, we went for ice-creams and that seemed to settle it.

Funnily enough though, he never asked for a *diabolo menthe* again.

Now while on the subject of ice-creams (I bet you were wondering where that was going) there's another tale to tell about the remarkable Sandy.

At that time, while we were living in Scotland, my role before opening up the office was to do the school run. Our kids went to a small village school just outside the town itself and there was no bus.

On these runs I always tried to entertain Calum and Sandy by talking about whatever came into my mind (and would not take more than ten minutes.) So one day I explained why humans can see in colour and many animals can't. This is because, I said, there are two types of vision receptor cells, rods and cones. Cones see colour and rods see brightness – monochrome, in other words. (I do know it's a bit more complicated than that, but these were primary kids.) Humans have both rods and cones, and many animals, like dogs, only have rods. So we see colour and they don't.

This went fine and was met with all the usual approval that could be mustered from a five-year old and an eight-year old.

I liked to test the little buggers to see if anything I said stuck, so a couple of days later I asked, 'Why do we see colour and dogs don't?'

To which Sandy, five, shouted out, 'Because they don't have any ice-creams in their eyes, only sticks!'

To which there was general hilarity. But he was still right.

I personally think my kids are all geniuses but I am quite certain Sandy is. That story, (which is true by the way) to me, serves to illustrate what genius really is; the ability to conceptualise an idea in a totally novel and unique way. All through his life, Sandy has been able to understand and describe the world in ways which are slightly – and some not so slightly – different from everyone else, yet which make perfect sense. And to his great credit, perhaps aided a little by his thoroughly anarchistic and non-conformist parents, he has maintained that unique and individual perspective.

Genius is not just being hugely intelligent, although it is partly that. Genius is being able to see the world in new ways, which allow different perspectives of understanding. Robert M Pirsig, in his novel *Zen and the Art of Motorcycle Maintenance,* talked of ideas as super-saturated solutions, clear liquid until a tiny speck of dust fell in. Then the whole would crystallise in instants, revealing structure, integrity, balance.

Genius is that speck of dust, the application of which causes a whole system of ideas to suddenly appear. And it takes minds unafraid to think differently to apply it. Da Vinci had it, Mozart had it, Newton had it, Darwin and Einstein had it. It's not given to everyone, but it is given to far more of us than we realise.

The trouble is that most children go through an education system that is not designed to make them celebrate their riotous, inchoate but absolutely brilliant minds. It is designed instead to snuff the sparkling flame of their unique vision and replace it with the dullness of the commonplace. We take the stuff of genius and turn it into the slurry of mere conformity, making fodder for the capitalist grist-mill and the patriarchal hegemony. We take our young minds and carefully, thoroughly, sanitise all the specks of precious dust. We teach our children how *not* to be geniuses.

One day we may have education systems that celebrate minds that conceptualise rods and cones as sticks and ice-creams. We might actually encourage people to think like that. We might reward innovation and iconoclasm and discourage the trotting out of conventional wisdom. We might devise education systems that not only allow young people to dare to be different, but which positively encourage it, that give out prizes for not being like all the others.

Perhaps one day we will have education systems, in other words, which exist for the benefit of both the students and humanity. Ones that don't exist for the convenience of career educators who make their living from the imposition of mind-numbing conformity. That are not arranged for the benefit of a corrupt politico-economic system determined to destroy the planet in the pursuit of quick money, or for the preservation of privilege, or the unquestioning maintenance of the status quo. Instead, we might have systems that produce genius.

But that seems a long way off, and this is meant to be amusing. Normal service will now be resumed.

Monsters in P'tit Moulin

Warning: if you replicate what I am about to describe and get yourself in bother, you're an idiot. You have been warned.

When we bought our dream house, the ground floor of the annexe (as we liked to call it) at the back was divided into two rooms and a corridor, all in a ghastly state. It was filthy and just...ugh. Horrible. The sort of thing you want to rub out and draw in again, as my brother used to say. And the floor was so damp it had mould growing. So that was going to have to be dug up.

I got out the Big Hammer and began knocking things down. I have always enjoyed that part. Very soon, the walls – which were of the thin French bricks plastered with gypsum, which just sponges up the damp – were demolished, shovelled into my trailer and then off to the communal tip. (We still had one of those then; not any more.)

This left a six by nine metre open space with an original oak staircase – in very bad state – in the corner. I carefully dismantled the lower part, not damaging any of the good timber, and set it aside. Most of the floor now exposed had been laid in hexagonal clay floor tiles called *tomettes*, with one section having already been lifted and concreted. The other areas were a mess because of the gaps where the walls had been.

There was a rather nice marble fireplace and a chimney above to begin with, but John, my then father-in-law, arrived during the demolition process and lent a hand. As I may have mentioned elsewhere, his enthusiasm in burning all the old timber and rubbish overheated the lintel of the fireplace so that it cracked and the whole bleeding lot collapsed. Well, at least I had a clear floor to work with.

I chiselled up the *tomettes* – don't let anyone ever kid you that lime mortar is easy to break – and dug out the infill below, which seemed to be mainly boiler slag and clinker. Apparently this was much used in the 19th century around here for jobs like this. I can assure you that it is horrible stuff to lift.

So, many trips to the tip later, I was ready to lay the new floor. First we put in some polystyrene sheets for insulation and then a plastic membrane.

I had set up a gang of pals to help on the big day and had a huge pile of concrete mix in the courtyard – all barrowed in from the road. We had two concrete mixers going and started at eight.

By the by, laying floors is one of the activities that really brings out the community spirit amongst the do-it-yourself-restore-an-old-wreck crowd in France. This is especially the case amongst the French themselves.

The thing is that anything wider than a two metre slab is a sod to lay on your own. A six by nine one would be a nightmare. You'd have to do it in sections and it would take a bleeding week. But nobody is going to hire labourers. That's against the rules and feeds into the system. So what happens is that Jacques, Yves and Joseph all agree to come and help Rod lay his floor, and Rod goes to help them when they lay theirs.

Works a treat; no extra costs, no taxes or charges, everybody gets a new floor.

Even better, this is France. So, we have to have lunch. The concrete-laying is therefore interrupted by a two-hour lunch break, where the host serves up the finest of fare, washed down with good red wine. And since laying floors is hard work and one does get thirsty, sufficient beer to lubricate the proceedings will be needed after lunch. (Before lunch coffee is appropriate; one should perhaps ensure that all the setting-out and levelling is done before noon too.)

I recall passing through a nearby village, where what looked like around four cubic metres of ready-mixed concrete had been dumped outside a house. Perspiration hailing off him, a doughty Frenchman was transporting it through a window in buckets before it set into a solid mini-Mont-Blanc on his doorstep.

I imagine his lunch provision must have been sub-par.

Anyway, *chez moi*, where lunch is always excellent, we were done by five and the serious beer-drinking could get under way. It was before the days when they enforced those pesky drink-driving laws, you understand.

And our annexe had a nice new concrete floor ready to tile.

Before the tiling, which we shall discuss presently, there was something else to attend to. The ceiling was in as much of a mess as the walls had been, although, to be fair, at least it wasn't damp. Part had been lath and plastered, but other parts showed the oaken *solives*, the floor joists between the massive main beams or *poutres*. These latter are 60 cm (24 inches) square by the way, lightly built this house is not. However the boards, the joists and the beams had all been painted in an assortment of finishes and colours, none of which was palatable at all.

It was pretty obvious that Something Would Have to be Done, so I began researching.

The standard method used at the time to strip paint from wood was a dry sand-blaster. I quickly discovered two things: they were incredibly expensive and had to be operated by a licensed operator because of the health risks; and they were filthy.

Did I want this sort of stuff in a house with one toddler and a new-born baby? My friend Antoine *le Potier* once again helped.

'They're horrible things,' he said. 'You used to be able to hire the machines alone but you can't now. Too dangerous.' He thought about it, looking at the ceiling. 'If that's just limewash it will probably come off with water.'

We finished our *aperos* and Antoine headed back to his studio, leaving me mulling this. Water? *Really?* So simple?

The next morning I got out the stepladder and prepared a bucket of hot water and a rag.

Antoine was right. Most of the paint was indeed limewash and it did come off with water. But it didn't come off easily. After about 45 minutes I had cleaned a tiny patch where I could see clean brown oak. But it was only about a foot (30cm) of floor joist. That ceiling is over fifty square metres. This would take weeks, and it was a horrible job, working over my head with filthy water running down my arm, under my sleeve, through my drawers and pissing out my trouser leg. I know now what it must be like to be incontinent.

Then there were the main beams, which had been painted, not with limewash but with proper oil paint. (Lime green.) That was completely immune to me and my bucket and rag. Somehow the thought of using paint stripper over my head was unappealing. Having my drawers full of dirty warm water was bad enough.

I put it aside to think it over and went to do something else, which probably, now I think on it, involved opening a bottle of wine..

As it always happened, a few days later I was at Antoine's for *aperos* and we got to talking about the ceiling. I told him of my success, but that it would take forever. His brow furrowed. 'What about a Karcher? You know, a pressure washer?'

I am so impressed by Antoine's lateral thinking ability sometimes. Remarkable man. I was awestruck.

'Yes…I mean there's nothing in there and it's summer. It would get a bit wet, but yes. It should work. But what about the oil paint?'

Antoine looked disappointed for a moment as he realised his brilliant scheme had a flaw. Then he grinned.

'Do you have three-phase?'

'What?'

'Electricity. You have three-phase?'

As it happened, we did, and I nodded. 'Yes, why.'

'Because my brother-in-law has a special Karcher. It has a wet sandblasting attachment and a boiler too.'

'You think he would lend it?'

'Oh yes, he doesn't use it. He bought it for washing his taxis but it's far too powerful. Takes the paint straight off. It's just sitting in his garage. I'll bet he'll even deliver it for you.'

Sure enough, two days later, Fred arrived in his Range Rover with a trailer on the back.

Special Karcher? I'll say. It was huge, and had a weird chimney arrangement.

'For the boiler,' he explained.

Although we had three-phase, we only had one three phase socket, which was down by the old storage heater in the grande Salle. But Fred had clearly thought ahead and had brought a 25-metre extension cable. We manhandled the Karcher – it weighed a ton – into the work area and hooked up the water and electricity. Then he showed me how to light the boiler, which ran on diesel. There was a temperature control for the water output; I set it to red and donned my protective goggles, which Fred told me were a must. The man himself retreated to a doorway where he could watch the shenanigans in shelter.

I was impressed by the recoil as I pulled the trigger on the lance and a jet of hot water blasted the ceiling. It was actually amazing, more like painting on clean wood than stripping off paint. In about ten minutes I had an area of perhaps a square metre completely clean. This was much more like it.

There was only one problem: The ceiling is 3 metres up and the splash-back had completely soaked me in warm, filthy water. Not only were my drawers soaked, all of me was.

Fred just laughed. 'You need a set of oilskins,' he chuckled. I bade him farewell for the moment, and after he'd left, thought about it. It was mid summer, the temperature was around 35 degrees. Furthermore, in just a few minutes of hot-water blast I had turned the room into a Turkish bath full of steam. Oilskins? In that heat? I'd faint.

I am pretty good at lateral thinking too. Why not just wear a pair of shorts? It was only lime and water, it wasn't harmful. Well a few centuries of dust, grime and spider's webs, but it wasn't, like poisonous or anything. I hoped.

So after lunch and a couple of glasses of wine, I suited up, or rather down.

Frankly I'd have done it naked but I was already aware that my actions in there were under observation from *Chez Angèle*, the cafe across the road, and I didn't want to provoke a health crisis. Angèle was getting on even then. So shorts it would have to be.

In the afternoon I launched myself at it and got along famously. Okay, I was black with hot wet grime, but a quick hose down in the courtyard afterwards and I was good as new, just ready for a little *blanc cassis*.

It took just over two days to strip the limewash off the whole ceiling, and then I had those pesky beams to do.

The Karcher, though, had the wet sandblasting attachment. This was much safer than the dry sort, since there would be no clouds of fine, possibly harmful dust. No need for a respirator suit, such as the dry sandblasters use.

I had bought, at huge expense, 125 litres of blasting sand. This was actually not sand at all but crushed glass, very sharp indeed.

The attachment just screwed into the end of the lance, and had feed pipe that you plunged into the tubs that the sand came in...Somewhat nervous, I got into position under a beam and let fly.

It was not as quick as the hot water on limewash, but it was still effective. However, the blasting grit was black, like carborundum and now, instead of being kind of a dirty grey colour, I was encrusted in black from head to foot, all except for the part round my eyes, where the goggles were.

Which was all right until I became aware that Moira standing in the doorway, gesticulating and yelling at me.

'There's someone at the door to see you!'

'Okay,' I replied and set down the lance. 'But I'll go through the barn, I'm too dirty to go through the house.'

Maybe I should have told her to prepare the unknown visitor for what was about to appear in the doorway: a six-foot, entirely jet-black hominid monster, dripping water, almost completely naked, wearing flip-flops with only two eyes showing. On my face, not the flip-flops. But I forgot.

My neighbour, who only wanted to borrow some tools, has looked at me a bit strangely ever since, and that was over twenty years ago.

The Tomettes

After weeks of work, our lovely back room, destined to be our *sejour*, was transformed. The old partition walls, made of *cloison brique*, had been reduced, in places, to a lattice of cement entirely free of brick, while in others the bricks that remained were so rotten that I could push my finger through. These had all been knocked down and the rubble taken to the tip. The old floor tiles had been lifted and sacked and a nice new, insulated concrete floor laid. The ceiling had been stripped of all paint with a pressure-washer, and thousands of nails had been pulled out using nippers. (It was a ghastly job, perhaps the worst of all.)

The new fireplace, lovingly constructed using the pillars we had half-inched from the derelict walnut oil mill, as described in *French Onion Soup!* was now constructed and a thing of wonder it was too.

We only needed one more thing to complete our delight: a tiled floor.

It had always been our intention to re-use the old tiles that I had so carefully lifted. These were (I hope you're listening) *tomettes* or traditional fired-clay tiles. They come in two different formats – square and hexagonal. Ours were hexagonal.

The problem with using old *tomettes* is that there were so many different manufacturers. Each of these made them in a slightly different size.

This is not too much of an issue if you're using large joints between the tiles but this is not at all the traditional way, at least not in Burgundy. Here, the tiles are butted up as close to each other as possible. No grout is used at all. The problem is that if any tiles of the wrong size are introduced, they prevent the proper tight joints. This is bad enough with square *tomettes*, and ten times worse with hexagonal ones, because the error spreads out in four directions. So you have to sort them very accurately and not mix them up.

Unfortunately I only had enough tiles lifted from that room to re-tile about two thirds of it. This was a real problem because the others we had were five millimetres larger, and there weren't enough of them to do the whole room either.

I was scratching my head about how I might deal with this and reading up all the books on traditional French floors that I could find, when, out of the blue, one of the neighbours dropped by. He announced he had just lifted 16 square metres of *tomettes* from one of his rooms and he wanted them out of his way.

I went to look, taking one of mine as a model, and Hallelujah! not only were they the same size, they were from the same manufacturer. (More recent *tomettes*, that is, those less than two hundred years old, were made in large commercial potteries and they have the maker's name and brand on the back.)

A *bidon* of wine changed hands and I began barrowing his *tomettes* round to my place.

Unfortunately, I was still about ten percent short of a full floor (and that was not a witticism about my mental state, although it might be true.)

What to do? I made dozens of drawings all with different potential solutions to this problem. Then one day, Moira and I were in a cafe in Chalon and we noticed the floor. Here, the *tomettes* had been laid inside squares made of oak. An idea began to form. The area of wood in such an arrangement might just be enough to let me finish the job with the *tomettes* I had.

I went to see my chum Antoine *le Potier*. Did he, I asked, have any suitable timber?

Yes, indeed he did. These were off-saw oak boards two metres long, nine centimetres wide and 27 millimetres thick.

'Just the job,' thinks I, a price was agreed and the deal doused in wine. (Of course.) Antoine even let me use his big planer-thicknesser to dress the timber; this was some time before I bought my own.

Now, I had a plan and some good drawings. I could progress.

Did you really think it was going to be that simple?

Gosh.

Anyway, whereas the *tomettes* I had lifted had come up fairly cleanly, my neighbour's had not. I had taken the time and trouble to loosen each individual tile with a bolster, while he had just attacked the floor with a pickaxe. So they'd come up sometimes four or five together, all attached to a lump of lime mortar. Nice. I mean, fair enough, he just planned to take them to the tip. He's not one for the traditional stuff, he prefers new (and ghastly) from Casto.

So I now had 16 square metres of *tomettes* that badly needed cleaning; and it's actually a lot more difficult to get the lime mortar off once they're up.

Well, I am a photographer, you see, old school. You know, actual chemicals. And I paid attention in chemistry (a knowledge I put to good use making IEDs, as they would now be called. I described this in a very funny book called *Poaching the River*.)

Therefore I know that hydrochloric acid is damn fine stuff for taking off lime. Unfortunately, this reaction produces chlorine gas – as used in the trenches, to dire effect.

With nowt else for it, off I hied to the local supermarket and bought 20 litres of HCl. In those days you could get the 48% stuff, which was good and strong; now you can only buy 23%.

Since it was still high summer I set up some trestle tables in the courtyard and a production line of baths – photographic trays. I arranged it so that the baths were rotated, weakest first, stronger and strongest. I didn't dilute, I just rotated, moving the baths along one and refilling the last with fresh acid as it became depleted.

The first thing to say about doing this is that yes, it really does produce chlorine gas and within minutes my eyes were streaming. It caught my throat so badly that I was obliged to drink copious amounts of beer to soothe it (yeah and I am sticking to that one, in case you were wondering.)

Moira came out, looked, coughed, waved her hand in front of her face and disappeared.

Once treated, the tiles were dumped in an old cast-iron bath in the courtyard (which is still there; it's a planter now.) It had a hose running fresh water into it and so rinsing the *tomettes*.

There are nearly a hundred tiles in a square metre, so the job took several days; but at the end I had a nice big stack of clean *tomettes* ready to lay.

During the evenings, I had set out my grid of timber that they would be laid inside. First, I fixed short timbers onto the concrete, and then I fixed the grid to those. This left about 50mm of height in which to fit the *tomettes* and a bed of cement mortar.

Once it was all set out and fixed, the laying began. It was slow work, mixing up the cement and laying them alone. But there was another wee problem.

You recall the floor I had seen in Chalon? Yes? Well, those were square *tomettes*. So they were easy. But I had – remember – hexagonal ones; which meant that each and every square had to have 19 (yes nineteen) *tomettes* cut to size. This was achieved in the traditional manner, using a nine-inch angle grinder with a diamond blade.

The upshot was that I could only do three or four square a day, so the laying took two weeks.

All in with the setting out, the machining and fixing of wood, the cleaning and laying of *tomettes*, the job took a month, full-time.

This seems a good moment to remind you of the worst failing of the do-it-yourself restoration artist: we never, ever, cost our time properly. Just be aware of that, should you ever tackle a job like this.

Anyway, with the tiles laid, the celebration could begin. We hit the champagne straight away but there was further fun to be had.

Once the floor had dried out – and by this time it was September – it had to be treated. I use the traditional method, raw linseed oil diluted with turps. We slathered a big bucket of this on the floor. Then a couple of old towels went down. And then Moira and I, dressed only in our underwear, proceeded to slide across the floor as if it were a skating rink, laughing hysterically and falling about, until the oil was properly spread out.

Goodness knows what the neighbours must have thought.

It is to my very great pride and satisfaction that my floor, laid nearly a quarter of a century ago now, remains just as beautiful today. Even more satisfying is that most of our visitors think that it is an original floor and are amazed when I tell them the truth.

Le Bol de Mariage

Marriage is a serious business, you know. Oh yes. A weighty and important decision that is meant to last for life – but increasingly rarely does.

Perhaps the surprising thing about marriage is that people, having once tried it and then – for reasons best known to themselves and also best left there – having decided to abandon the project, at massive expense, including loss of property, money and, of course, being obliged to pay fortunes to money-grubbing specimens of the legal trade – actually go and do it again. Sometimes more than once.

It is a phenomenon of more than passing curiosity.

I actually stopped going to weddings about twenty-five years ago, largely on religious grounds. I just found it offensive that I should be asked to pass for a believing person when that is quite honestly the very last thing I am...well maybe not the very last, but near enough, you know.

Which will make the last part of this chapter all the more interesting, I do believe.

Marriage in France is not quite as it is in the Isle of the tarnished and hocked Sceptre. France, deliciously, has a constitutional separation between Church and State, whereas England (not Scotland) is technically a theocracy, with its head of State, the reigning monarch, being also the head of the Established Church of England.

This was, by the way, why the English spent so many years rooting priests out from their priest holes and burning them alive. By not converting to Henry VIII's pretendy church, Catholics were committing treason. This is why Guido Fawkes – you do remember him, don't you – tried so hard to do us all a favour and blow up Parliament. Later commentators have got this all wrong; he wasn't trying to hoist the Parliamentarians, he was trying to launch the King – James the VI and I – into outer space. Which, if you ever study the history of said Monarch, you might agree would have been his just come-uppance. Or *blow*-uppance. Ho ho.

In general I will defend Scotland, Scots and all things Scottish, but even I would have to admit that James VI was a warped, perverted, nasty, little, erm, king. To boot (gasp) I am a confirmed republican (small 'r' for you Septics) and hoisting the wearer of the golden hat seems...well, it would have been so much more stylish than the Yekaterinburg solution, where you round up the incumbent and all his offspring into a sealed basement and then shoot them. That always seemed, to me, to lack self-confidence and vim, you know? And beheading is so *passé*, don't you think? I mean, all those *heads*.

Launching the bugger skywards, still attached to his throne atop a sheet of flame, accompanied by a deafening explosion and mushroom clouds of smoke, now that's the way to do it. Shows a real grasp of Public Relations and the value of a great news image. And to boot, it would have liberated a prime piece of real estate, albeit occasionally prone to flooding, on which one could have built the most super-duper mall thingy.

So I quite admire old Guido. I think he could have done us all a great favour.

Meantime back to the plot; one must not wax excessive lyrical, must one? Where was I? Oh yes, marriage. Tried it once. No comment.

Because of the aforementioned separation of Church and State, religious marriages in France have no legal value. All such unions must be ratified by the representative of said Glorious Republic, who is – can't you guess – the local mayor. Well I understand he deputises in the large cities, otherwise the poor man would never be done hitching, but in the small towns and villages, it's the ordinary mayor – who is also by definition the Justice of the Peace and official solemniser of legal documents.

Anyway the normal practice is for the couple to go through the civil wedding before the churchy one. Which is nice and logical and as you know, the French they like logical.

I wonder if you noticed something else? Well it's like this.

Naturally both bride and groom must have their shower, stag night, hen night, whatever you might like to call it. This is a session of unbridled, alcoholically-fuelled debauchery, before the wedding. So that means the night before the civil ceremony.

After the civil ceremony, the couple are legally wed, so of course, they must have a party. Goes without saying.

The next day, after the church wedding, there will obviously be *another* party, and this will be a serious one, like. The previous two were just softening you up. This is where it gets messy. And finally, there will be the clearing up and sorting out, the returning of hired glasses and whatnots and whatever else to do the next day, all with the most ferocious hangovers imaginable – which requires yet another party to eat

Croutons and Cheese!

and drink up all the leftovers.

So you see, since the favourite hitching day is Saturday, the favoured *invitées* will enjoy four solid days of revelry and gastronomic orgy.

It will take your liver a month to recover, trust me.

Now French weddings are as replete with quaint little customs as they are everywhere; and remember, I am Scottish, so I'm used to weird habits. These include Lowlanders dressing up like 19th century Highland lairds and attempting to throw screaming girls out windows, or at least, across the dance floor. I am no stranger to bizarre conventions.

By the by, and now I think on it, I recently came across, on a USican website, an apparently ancient Scottish tradition called 'the Kirking of the Tartan'. This, it seems, is a necessary precursor to the official hitching, after which the leg-over is sanctioned. Where *do* they get their ideas from, these colonial scamps? Nobody in Scotland ever heard of such utter twaddle. Brigadoonery to the max.

Here in P'tit Moulin, just recently we had our first wedding in five years. When I think back and remember how many there used to be, it is a little sad. But this one went off a storm. As is pretty normal, the happy couple already had three kids, so they all accompanied Mum up the aisle. It was a lovely moment.

Coming out, the bride and groom had to walk through a tunnel of shotguns held high, long fireworks doing the same thing, and footballs, also held aloft. As they passed under, the shotguns were discharged and the fireworks lit. Meantime the footballs were bounced up and down in a very suggestive manner.

I leave the reader to surmise the symbolism; let's just say that weddings in P'tit Moulin may be rare now but they do not want for earthiness.

Anyway, amongst all the French marriage customs, which mainly seem to have to do with eating far too much, drinking even more, and references to the act of sex, there is one that I thought might *enchant* you.

Many years ago I was invited to the wedding of close friends in Nuits St Georges. The programme of events was much as I have outlined, a lad's night on Thursday (and the same for the distaff), a decent bender on the Friday and then the Big Daddy on the Saturday.

Some hours into this last, I became aware that the happy couple had vanished and I put two and two together. I was trying my best (with some success I might add) to woo a desperately cute little French bundle named Annie. So I really didn't care where the married couple had gone to or what they were up to, except insofar as I had every intention of doing something similar with the bewitching brunette beside me.

Suddenly Annie came over all agitated and broke from the closeness we had adopted. I was aware that she was getting ready to leave. This was not at all what I had been planning, so I was a bit concerned.

'What's going on?' quoth I.

'*Vite, vite, depeche-toi,*' says she. 'We 'ave to 'unt zem now.'

I was, I admit, a little, erm, well refreshed, but hey, I wasn't driving. I really couldn't imagine that my fellow guests would either, but how wrong I was. We all – well, everyone under thirty-five (this was a while ago, you understand) – made our way out of the *salle des fêtes* that had been hired for the bash and into the parking lot. Five of us piled into Annie's *Deux Chevaux* – no really I am not making this up, everybody French had one of those back then – in a fairly uncontrolled state of hysteria.

'*Depechez-vous,*' ordered Annie, jamming the car into reverse before I had even closed the door, and backing out of the parking place on two wheels – a surprisingly easy feat in a 2CV. Of course nobody wore seat belts then.

She accelerated after a line of cars leaving the car park.

'Where are we going?' I ventured. (Hysterical giggles from back seat.)

'We 'ave to find zem. Zey are 'iding somewhere.' (Hysteria.)

The line of cars – every one wearing out its horns – sallied out. The klaxonade was accompanied by a fusillade, as a previously unnoticed stash of bangers was launched out of car windows. I could clearly see the car behind had a shotgun poking through its sunroof – it was the groom's cousin – and it was being fired too. It wasn't the only one either.

I am positive we passed along the same stretches of road several times. After ten minutes or so, the convoy stopped at a local hotel and everyone got out. After searching the place – to the huge amusement of the staff, who, I was later informed, had been prepped – we drew a blank and off into the night again, horns blasting. There was constant hysteria from the back seat of Annie's car. There were three girls there whom I had only met in passing, cousins of the bride or something. I'm amazed they didn't wet themselves.

This procedure carried on for a couple more hotels; then at the last one, Annie stayed in the car.

'Why are we not going in?' I asked (Hysteria from behind.)

'Because zey are not 'ere.' (Convulsions.)

I looked at her in astonishment. She shrugged 'Lise is my best friend. Of course I knew all along where zey went. It's just a game, you know?' (Hysteria.)

'Is that why they can't stop laughing?' (Whatever is more hysterical than hysteria. They were crying now.)

She shook her head. 'No, it's because zey 'ave ze *bol de mariage.*' (More hysteria, protracted this time.)

'But it's time to go zere now. It's late and I am bored.' She squeezed my hand. 'Zere are other things we could be doing.' We kissed again and there was serious ribaldry from the back seat, so we cut off short, grinning, as those who both plan some deeper intimacy as soon as a quiet place can be found, do. 'So zis time I will lead. Zat's why we don' get out of ze car.' (Again the hysteria.)

Sure enough, as the others came of the hotel, Annie drove to the head of the column of cars, and soon we roared off, rattling and blasting, tooting, and fusillading like the OK Corral, through country lanes, till we came to an isolated *auberge.* Annie pulled up and switched off the motor. 'Zey are 'ere,' she giggled.

We got out. and our three passengers retrieved an object covered in a cloth from the boot. I was aware that we were now at the centre of a large crowd.

'Let's go,' said Annie, and we went into the *auberge,* where monsieur *le patron* was grinning like a cat, waiting for us. He presented Annie with a magnum of champagne in an ice-bucket and leaned forward, saying a few words into her ear. She thanked him and we made our way up the stairs.

My friends, the recently (twice) married Jacques and Lise were safely tucked up in bed, he bare-chested and she in a negligée. But the atmosphere was more ribald than romantic. Our three hysterical passengers made their way to the front and took the cloth off the mysterious object. Laughing out loud, Annie poured the champagne into it, and they turned and held aloft the item for the delight of all.

It was a porcelain chamber-pot with melted chocolate dribbled all over it. To complete the illusion, it had toilet paper stuck to the sides – and was now filled with champagne. Hilarity was now general and intense; so much so that my sides were beginning to ache.

With mock formality, Annie passed the pot to Jacques, who quaffed deep, to hoots and boisterous shrieks. French weddings are not quiet affairs. Then Lise did the same, to a similar response.

The chocolate-smeared chanty (I told you you'd be enchanted) was then passed around the assembled company and we all drank, to much laughter, claps on backs and general ribaldry.

After about fifteen minutes the ceremony came to an end and we withdrew, leaving the married couple to their first night of formally sanctioned passion. Annie and I repaired to her place for something similar – but that might have to be another story.

This was before I met Moira, you understand.

Postscript.

As I write this, it is just over twenty-three years since I drove down from Ivry, with the fat Notary sweating at my side and mopping his brow. We breasted the hill to the east and for the first time laid eyes on the umber softness of the village that would come to mean so much to us. I remember seeing, from afar, the church spire, the *relais de la poste,* and the house that was to become our own precious dream. We fell in love there and then with the ochre and terra-cotta buildings, the green and lush fields around, and the dreaming tranquillity, the golden light, the azure sky.

So much has changed now, though the honeyed hues of summer have not, thankfully. P'tit Moulin is as charming and idyllic, as rustic and quaint as it ever was. But the life is ebbing from it, little by little. The Post Office and the village shop have closed, finally and definitively.

There are no church services on Sundays now, only the rare ones that signal that another of the dwindling number of sons of the soil has hopped the mortal twig.

Kiki *la Gare* is dead. So is *le* Robert, along with his lifelong friend Monsieur Poulot. The old woman with the fruit is no longer here, nor is her husband. *Le* Stephan is gone and the old mayor, the father of the present one, passed this year. There are but three *anciens combattants* these days. There is no longer a great *spectacle* on *Quattors Juillet* and few children now play in the churchyard in the summer. Most evenings P'tit Moulin is like a ghost town.

Even *Chez Angèle*, that bubbling hub of local intelligence, where I first met the Moulinards and where Jean-Pierre the homosexual played his daily joke, flouncing in and out in silk gown and slippers, is no more. I went for my usual bottle of wine earlier this year – having been away for some months – to find that it was no longer sold. The cafe has closed and with it, this being France, the heart of the village has stopped beating. The last of the merry band who frequented it must have found another establishment; they no longer urinate against Angèle's barn doors, anyway.

Nearly all of the *grandes dames* are dead and with them their husbands, the horny-handed sons of the soil whose faces I shall carry to my own grave. A few remain, but most have passed the farms on to their own sons, or sold up to one of the farmers turned agri-businessmen. It is as it is; nobody wants to be a peasant farmer; and who on earth could blame them? Our mayor – ever charming – is not a farmer, though he be the son of one. He is an agri-economical consultant. He drives a sports car and wears Yves St Laurent. His new *amour* is a city girl: refined, sexy and much younger than his ex-wife is.

The school struggles on, but its future is reviewed every year and the schoolmistresses, while charming, are not part of village life. They come and they go, modern commuters. Even the grocery van that used to come three times a week, bringing provender to the village, has stopped. The driver, I am sad to report, died.

The lugubrious Pete and the neurotic Sharon have long since departed; they live near Cluny now, in an isolated house that is close to no-one. It will suit them better. Sharon may even have found her idyll of *Manon des Sources*. Pete, I am sure, will be more content, now that his beloved is happy.

Antoine *le Potier*, like me, is grey-haired these days, and teaches at the local Art School. He has normalised his life and his marvellous wood-fired kiln, that magical confection of pyrotechnical awe, has lain dismantled and unused these last fifteen years.

For me, too, so many changes. Moira and I are no longer married; we separated and later divorced. The children are grown up and live in Scotland; they rarely visit this old eyrie in the Arrière-côte. And as with Mahomet, since the mountain will not come to me, then I must needs go to it.

I have lived here in P'tit Moulin for, in total, more than ten years. It perhaps doesn't seem so many, after six decades on this Earth; but so many memories were made in those years! Crammed full of experience, raw, hot from the great press of life.

Lately, however, I have spent increasingly longer periods in the Philippines. I can no longer stand the cold and dark of winter in Europe and to be alone during these months is purgatory. And in any case, in rediscovering Asia, I have discovered a new world, one which I wish to explore, before it is too late; I am now sixty and a realist.

I might drift into slumber before my stove, allowing the dust to settle on and around me like a carapace, becoming a part, in the end, of the fabric of this ancient house. I could wait tranquilly for the last long night to catch up with me. But that old call is still there, that plaintive wailing over the moors at dusk. It is the call of the road, and no-one who hears it can resist. It is the siren-song of life itself calling us into the unknown.

There are only two sorts of people: those who hear that call and follow and those who do not hear it at all.

In a way, that has been the love of P'tit Moulin. The people here do not hear that song. If they did they would have left, as so many did, to new lives and futures elsewhere. And there are some who have heard it, and have followed, but whose tumbleweed stopped rolling when it fetched up here. These people succour us, we inveterate wanderers. We thrive vicariously on the bubbles of love they create. We know that they have chosen – wittingly or not – limitations that we never could live with; but it feels good to be surrounded by them. They protect us from that eldritch banshee's wail, which strikes such terrible chill into our hearts.

You see, like Frodo Baggins, we never wanted to be wanderers. Nobody gave us a choice. We are as we are and the die was cast for us. When I was seven years old and set out for London with a few biscuits tied in a handerchief and suspended from a stick over my shoulder, my mother knew how it was. She caught up with me near the road to Hunter's Path, a mile from our gate.

'Wanderlust, Roddy,' she said. 'You'll never be rid of it.' She knew it because she had it and so did her mother, though, as women and mothers, they had been controlled in their desire.

We, the rootless ones, love the settled, their golden lives, the voices of their children, the smell of the fresh bread they make, the idea of living out our days in one place, of dreams fulfilled and lifelong companionship. And nearly all of us try hard to replicate that for at least a part of our lives.

We will try to drive the road out by mimicking the happy settled people around us. It is as if by pretending to be like them, we could become so.

Such a solution is doomed to failure by our natures. We are not dogs, but cats. We might yearn to be dogs and play with them, but we can never truly be *of* them.

Frodo, his great adventure over, could not linger in the Shire. It is as it is; a wanderer but rarely settles and those who do, mark you, will always regard us with even greater suspicion than the others. After all, most people neither love nor fear the road. It's just a way to get to town, for them. For us, it's life itself; and no-one is more tempted than the settled wanderer. He is the addict in remission.

So we are attracted to the settled and we stay by them, drawing in the warmth of their love. But only for a time. Sooner or later, the windows open and smelling the wind from the West, or seeing the scuttering leaves swirl and eddy in the autumn breeze, we know. It is time to pack. And we cannot resist.

The call of the road, the siren-song of the new, the fascination with what might possibly just be around yonder bend, these are my temptations. They always have been. And though I love books, they have never been enough. I have always needed total immersion; the burn of experience. I am a cutting-edge junky, hooked on the high of the new. I always have been; and I am much too old to change now. I once thought I could and I tried hard enough; now I know that I was wrong. Nobody can.

Coming here, everything I have done, throughout my own journey, has only been to follow that call, to seek that immersion, to put my hand over that flame.

When I was a child, there were still tramps in Scotland. My mother told me to stay away from them. Like most who know the scent of the West Wind, she mistrusted the itinerant, but not because she feared that they might rob her. It was becuase of the sympathetic vibrations they set off in her own soul, the triggering of the wanderlust.

I, even as a boy, was fascinated by the idea; to spend a life wandering, just experiencing the new, every day. I do not doubt that is a romanticised and childish notion, but it is what I am, the educated tramp who wanders the planet, not aimlessly but without direction. My mother called it 'following her nose'; and the lovely Burgundian writer Henri Vincenot called it *La Billebaude*. All I can say is that, in truth, I have never had any other goal than to grasp that which was just beyond my reach.

I should also say, to anyone who recognises their inner tramp, their wayward soul that will be as quickly be off on some new adventure, that hates the slow silting up of arteries that comes with familiarity: do not fight it, my friend. Follow and embrace it.

If you do, you will find us everywhere. We are your *companions de la route*. Just as Frodo and Sam did, we set out, our packs on our backs, our feet on the road, and no clue when we will return, or if indeed we ever shall. We will know you, and you shall know us.

I have no plans to sell our dream home in France, but that is partly because the thought of dealing with the mountains of stuff I have acquired is more than I can find the strength to countenance. And despite my wanderlust, there is a part of me that is conservative, that adjures me to hold on to some little corner of planet Earth that is my own.

Foolish, for all of that planet is mine, but too tempting to resist. Like my mother, whom I come to resemble more with each passing year, I ever try to juggle my conflicting spirits, that which would follow a will o' the wisp and that which ever seeks to hunker down in its den.

I think I shall always return here, but I know now that it was a part of my journey, not the destination. There is no destination. I am a wanderer; I am like a donkey assiduously pursuing a carrot on a stick, forever just out of reach and too tempting to ignore.

I am often asked what the difference is between a traveller and a tourist. I have all sorts of stock responses about package holidays, about finding out the 'real place'. But it's not that at all. The answer is simple: like a tramp, a traveller doesn't *go* anywhere. He just travels. In cars, on motorcycles, in planes, boats and trains. He is supertramp. By accident, he arrives at interesting places. And he never goes home, because he has none. His home is just where he hangs his hat.

Do not let my pragmatism make you underestimate my love for P'tit Moulin. This place has meant, and means, more to me than I can say. I have spent so many evenings in our perfumed courtyard here, watching the bats as the gathering dusk went from blue to indigo to velvety darkness. I have watched the criss-crossing trails of jetliners flying in and out of Lyon catch the light of sunset, casting a net of gold across the sky. I have gazed as first the planets, then the stars, began to glimmer, and, as the full night drew on and the streetlights went out, wondered at the majesty of the Milky Way, its magnificent luminosity arching above me. And then I remember that I too am stardust; that is where I came from, and that is where I shall return. I do not feel sad at this: I have lived my life to the full and such a life have I lived!

P'tit Moulin will never leave me and I shall never fully leave it. I am a part of its history now. I have laughed here and I have cried, too.

It is love, not location, that counts. Love is the only thing that matters. My mind turns, now, to the Gallo-Roman stele in the church. There is a memento to love a millennium and a half old. It seems a fitting place to end.

And so, in the darkling crepuscule, it appears that we have come to a crossroads. I bid thee farewell, my companion, at least for now. My path leads me yonder and yours must take you back to the warmth of your home and the comfort of your bed. I hope my tales have amused and entertained you; brightened a little your own journey. I shake your hand and doff my hat. I trust we shall meet again, in some other adventure. May you love and be loved, and your life be full. And in the evening of your days, may your wanderer find peace.

Au revoir.

P'tit Moulin, September 2016

The End

About Me

Picture: Charis Fleming

I am a Scottish photographer, multimedia artist and writer, with a long career as a freelance journalist and photographer.

I write books on a variety of topics in both fiction and non-fiction. I remain active as a writer, photographer, printmaker and publisher.

I graduated with Bachelor of Art with Honours from Edinburgh College of Art in 1983, majoring in sculpture and also pursuing life-drawing, printmaking and film-making.

After graduation I worked in film-making before returning to photography. During this time I also pursued Journalism Studies through Napier University in Edinburgh.

For decades, both as a photographer and Picture Editor, I presented the readers of the newspapers and magazines I worked for, as well as many disparate clients, with the very best of photographic imagery.

After publishing news and feature articles for many years, I began to write more intensely in the 1990s. My first book, *Poaching the River,* was published in 2006.

In 2009 I published my second full-length book, *The Warm Pink Jelly Express Train.*

I fulfilled an ambition I had held for many years and graduated with a Master of Fine Art degree from Dundee University in 2011, where my practical area was photography and printmaking, especially photogravure, and my Dissertation was on Goddess culture.

At the end of 2011 I returned to France and began to focus more on writing. In 2013 I published the first book in this series, *French Onion Soup!*

Books by Rod Fleming

French Onion Soup! ISBN: 978-0-9565007-3-1

The first book in this series, *French Onion Soup!* tells you about about arriving in France, wine, food, the *affouage*—a unique way of gathering winter fuel—French lawyers, renegade mules and many other areas of Burgundian life, in a quirky and hilariously funny style.

A Little Shop of Horors. ISBN: 978-0-9565007-8-6

Creeps and chills from a selection of modern horror stories guaranteed to make you think twise about turning out the light. Most are set in Scotland with authentic background details and tap into the rich folklore of the country. Just right for a winter evening!

Why Men Made God. ISBN: 978-0-9572612-2-8

The Egyptians, Greeks, Romans, Celts and northern Europeans all had pantheons of gods and goddesses. What changed and led to the idea of just one, all-powerful God? Why was the original Goddess abandoned in favour of a sequence of sky-fathers? Who wrote the Bible and why? What impact does that have on us today?

Why Men Made God answers these questions, in a pacy and easy-to-read manner, backed up with science. With Karis Burkowski.

Fiction

The Warm Pink Jelly Express Train. ISBN: 978-0-9572612-3-5

Brian Macmaster is a journalist licking the wounds of a divorce in Paris. He meets a transsexual prostitute who leads him into a spider's-web of intrigue, deception and extortion. *The Warm Pink Jelly Express Train* is a sexy, powerful, relentlessly paced novel that is not only a page-turner but also explores one of the most fascinating taboos of contemporary culture.

A Kiss for Christmas. ISBN: 978-0-9565007-7-9

Christmas 1981: Europe is in turmoil, the *Human League* is top of the charts, it's pissing stair-rods in Paris and Johnny MacFarlane has just got back from Damascus with a load of smuggled blood diamonds.

Harry, the most notorious fence in Paris, offers him a special surprise: Hermann Goering's gold-plated 9mm Luger. Johnny goes back to the bar to pay his tab, when he gets another surprise: a bullet. That's when his world explodes.

The Children of Aldebaran. ISBN: 978-0-9572612-1-1

The time of the Big People is past and the world is ruled by the Animals. Silas Farsight, a young otter who looks forward to a life as a lawyer in the forest village, is horrified when his cousin is kidnapped by a gang of ferocious cats. With his indentured clerk Stoatwise Cuttleworth, he sets off in pursuit.

His cousin, Magda, is being taken to the Dark City, where an evil beast known as the Great Cat is plotting imperial domination of the Free Animals. Silas must rescue her. His adventures lead him to the Sea Otters, a wild and mysterious people, of whom he knows only myth and legend. Yet it is with them that he will find his own true destiny. A fast-paced and exciting fantasy adventure.

Poaching the River. ISBN: 978-0-9554535-0-2

It's a typical sleepy afternoon in Auchpinkie, a tiny fishing village on the east coast of Scotland. But all that's about to change. The action races to its riotous climax, as local hero Big Sandy poaches the River Pinkie in a daring adventure, the public convenience is destroyed by a freak explosion, and the minister is baffled by the sudden religious conversion of two formerly heathenish young lads. *Poaching the River* will make you laugh and cry out loud.

The Spring Run. ISBN: 978-0-9572612-5-9

Spring is coming to the village of Auchpinkie on the east coast of Scotland. With it, women's minds turn to romance and men's to something else — poaching. But it turns out these are actually very closely related. *The Spring Run* is a hilarious and charming romantic comedy set in a world full of larger-than life characters. (This is a standard-English translation of *Poaching the River.*)

Buying

You can buy my books as paperbacks or as e-books from any good retailer in most of the world, including Amazon, Barnes & Noble, Waterstones and all major e-book retailers.

Alternatively, please navigate to my site at http://rodfleming.com/ where you will find direct links to purchase them online or by digital download.

Visit my Amazon author page!

https://www.amazon.com/author/rodfleming

www.ingramcontent.com/pod-product-compliance
Lightning Source LLC
Chambersburg PA
CBHW052019290426
44112CB00014B/2306